Know Your White Superlock

Know Your White Superlock

by Naomi Baker and Tammy Young

Chilton Book Company

Radnor, Pennsylvania

Published in Radnor, Pennsylvania
19089, by Chilton Book Company

Cover Design by Tony Jacobson
Designed by Martha Vercoutere
Color Photographs by Lee Phillips
Illustrations by Chris Hansen

Manufactured in the United States of
America

Library of Congress Cataloging in
Publication Data

Baker, Naomi
    Know your White Superlock /
Naomi Baker and Tammy Young.

    p. cm.—(Creative machine arts
series)
    Includes index.
    1. Serging I. Young, Tammy.
    II. Title. III. Series.
TT713.B3325 1991   90-55878
646.2'044—dc20   CIP
ISBN 0-8019-8107-7

1 2 3 4 5 6 7 8 9 0   0 9 8 7 6 5 4 3 2 1

Contents

Preface

A little over a decade ago, sergers (or as they're sometimes called, overlock machines) appeared on the home-sewing market. Most sergers at that time were industrial models—big, noisy, difficult to operate, with dangerous knives, and always breaking down.

But home-sewing serger models were a very different piece of equipment than their industrial cousins. They've been domesticated, with practically all the advantages and few of the drawbacks.

Small, clean, quiet, and safe, sergers now give us creative possibilities that previously were not available to the home-sewer. During the last decade, enthusiasts have taken serger sewing from a few basic stitches and techniques to a wide variety of decorative applications and innovative uses. We call the latest developments in decorative serger sewing **ornamental serging.**

As the publisher and consulting editor of the *Serger Update* newsletter and co-authors of three serging books published by Chilton Book Company, we have been in a unique position to witness firsthand the exciting developments in the art of serger sewing. New equipment, technology, and notions have opened up more and more possibilities for creativity.

The White Sewing Machine Company, manufacturer of *White Superlock* sergers, has been a leader in creative serging education. White has sponsored shows, produced extensive written material and videos, and furthered interest in decorative serger sewing.

Know Your White Superlock is meant to encourage you to join in this exciting trend, taking you beyond the basics and encouraging you to explore uses for the serger as an artistic instrument. We will outline methods for seaming, edge finishing, binding and trimming, and other decorative serging techniques. Simple projects are included at the end of every lesson to demonstrate skills. These projects are excellent for quick gifts as well as for hands-on teaching.

We hope this book will encourage you to join the world of ornamental serging. Your handy *Superlock* will execute the basics beautifully. But taken one step further, it can easily make all of your serging projects one-of-a-kind creations.

So breeze through the basics (if you haven't already), and begin to look at all the creative serging options.

Happy ornamental serging,
Naomi Baker and Tammy Young

Foreword

Those of us lucky enough to own a serger need no convincing that as an invention, it ranks right up there with Post-it Notes, rotary cutters, and the microwave.

Yet those of us brave enough to tell the whole truth will confess that we've barely scratched the surface of our serger's capabilities.

I'm no different. Though I'm devoted to my serger, I've used it primarily to clean finish seam allowances. I'd like to do more, but my time for experimenting is limited. What I need is a master teacher at my side, coaxing me to twirl those knobs, change that thread, try this technique.

Shazam! Not one, but two master teachers have appeared through a puff of smoke. Tammy and Naomi, in the pages of this book, are exactly what you and I need. They walk us through the basics, and then lesson by lesson, teach a new technique, ending with a sample project using that technique. Some of my favorite ornamental serging techniques are the serged frog closure, elastic button loops, and double-bound seams.

For a busy sewer, this lesson format is ideal. You can try a lesson in an evening, make a sample for your notebook, then choose your favorite techniques to embellish a garment on the weekend.

By the time you finish, you will truly know your serger.

Robbie Fanning
Series Editor

Are you interested in a quarterly newsletter about creative uses of the sewing machine, serger, and knitting machine? Write to The Creative Machine-ws, PO Box 2634, Menlo Park, CA 94026.

Acknowledgments

This book would not have been possible without the full cooperation and assistance of the White Sewing Machine Company, manufacturer of *White Superlock* sergers. Special thanks to Sue Hausmann, Nancy Jewell, and the entire company management team for their enthusiastic support.

Thank you also to our professional "Serger Update" writers and other industry professionals who have pioneered serger sewing and inspired us.

We also want to thank the talented people who have helped us immeasurably in producing this book: Chris Hansen, illustration; Lee Phillips, photography; Martha Vercoutere, book design; and Lori Bottom, manuscript preparation.

Finally, many thanks go to our editor, Robbie Fanning, and our publisher's representative, Kathryn Conover, for believing in our efforts and encouraging us to write a series of brand-specific books on ornamental serging techniques.

The following are registered trademark names used in this book: *Candlelight, Decor 6, Fabric Mender Magic, Fray Check, Lycra, OK to Wash-It, Perfect Pleater, Ripstop, Seams Great, Solvy, Stiffy, Superlock, TAC Spray Stiff, Teflon, Thinsulate, Ultrasuede, Velcro, Wash-Away,* and *Wonder-Under*.

1. Superlock Basics

- **Bonding with Your Serger**
- **Serging and Sewing Strategies**
- **How to Use This Book**
- ***Superlock* Features**
- ***Superlock* Stitch Formation**
- ***Superlock* Feet and Accessories**
- **Loving Care**

Bonding with Your Serger

The biggest hurdle to overcome in the exciting adventure of serger sewing is **taking the machine out of the box.** Yes, that's right! Over the years, we've found that for many home-sewers, the serger looked wonderful when demonstrated in the store. It was capable of speedy seaming, pretty rolled edges, and all sorts of decorative techniques. But when the home-sewer brought it home, the serger seemed daunting and complicated. (After all, it's an entirely different kind of machine than the sewing machine we all have known.) So into the closet it goes, just waiting for that rainy day when there's plenty of time to figure out how to use it and to practice all of those wonderful serger techniques.

Of course, the longer the serger stays in the closet, the more complex and intimidating it seems. Meanwhile, your "friendly" sewing machine is right there to fall back on.

The next hurdle in serger use occurs when we do take the machine out of the box, and the dealer has adjusted it for a perfectly balanced seam. We can serge beautifully balanced seams and edges, but heaven forbid that we might have to switch to a rolled edge or a flatlock. Horrors! That can involve taking out a needle, changing a foot and plate, and adjusting the tension settings. The thought of tackling all these separate steps seems overwhelming at first.

But just stop and consider how many different adjustments you make effortlessly on your sewing machine—winding the bobbin, threading, changing needles and feet, making stitch-length adjustments, and converting to special stitches. The serger only seems complicated at first, when we're getting used to it and to its unique method of sewing.

There's a simple answer. Take your serger out of the box, read the owner's instruction manual, and practice the various kinds of stitches available on your model. In other words, ***use your serger and you'll become comfortable with it sooner than you think.***

Serger expert Sue Green calls this process "bonding." Although the term is most often used for parents' feeling toward their child or for other personal relationships, it applies nicely to serger sewing as well. As you spend more time with your machine and get to know it, you will learn its idiosyncrasies, talents, and personality. At varying times this bonding process can be frustrating, exciting, intimidating, or rewarding—and just plain fun. Sharpening your spirit of adventure can be a big help.

If serging classes are available to you, by all means take advantage of them. They're a great way to speed up the learning process, pick up tips and techniques, and have a good time in the process.

In this book, we assume that you have already learned the basics of serger sewing. Check the following list to be sure.

___ Threading
___ Changing and balancing tension
___ Changing stitch width and length
___ Adjusting for a rolled edge (Practice until you can do it effortlessly.)
___ Adjusting for flatlocking
___ Using the differential feed
___ Changing needles
___ Cleaning your machine—and oiling it
___ Clearing the stitch finger
___ Serging inside and outside corners
___ Ripping out stitches

Your instruction manual is a must. If you don't have one, buy or order one from your dealer. The manual contains detailed instructions on the basics listed above. Work your way through the manual early in your bonding process.

In addition to your manual, extensive information is available to lead you through all the machine basics and construction techniques and beyond. (Several excellent resources are listed under Other Publications by the Authors.) For most *Superlock* models, an owner's workbook and instructional video are also available.

When sergers were first introduced in the United States, their use was limited to simple seams and edge finishes. Since then, serger sewing enthusiasts have developed a great deal of exciting new information. As you get to know your serger and put it to work, you will discover a whole new world of ornamental serging possibilities.

Serging and Sewing Strategies

Your serger is a natural companion to your sewing machine. Rather than working in competition with each other, these two machines team up to offer us endless possibilities. Once you are familiar with your serger and all its potential uses, you will soon know when to use your sewing machine and when to use your serger for any project or parts of a project.

The serger is fast, finishes edges beautifully, makes neat, sturdy seams, and replicates many of the looks found in today's couture and ready-to-wear. It efficiently sews many specialty fabrics we would have hesitated to tackle in the past, including sheers, silkies, and loosely wovens. The built-in stretch of a serger stitch also makes serging a favored option for interlocks, *Lycra* blends, and sweatering.

We've often heard that the serger speeds up sewing, that it trims, seams, and overlocks in one step, that it makes beautiful rolled edges and has many decorative uses. But the one thing we don't always hear is that **serger sewing is all about edges.**

Because the loopers must go above and below the fabric in order to form an overlock stitch, most serging must necessarily be done on edges or folds. (Fig. 1-1)

upper looper

lower looper

edge or fold

Fig. 1-1: *Because of a serger's looper mechanism, always place serging on an edge or fold.*

The serger's ability to sew on edges includes seams (see Chapter 3), flatlocking (in Lessons 3 and 25), and edge finishing (discussed in Chapter 4). Beyond these basics, interesting variations abound.

The sewing machine, unlike the serger, has the ability to sew anywhere on a piece of fabric, not just on an edge or fold. Its straight-stitch capability—for top-stitching and edge-stitching—is essential to supplement many serger techniques. Also, its decorative stitches can be combined with serging to enhance your creativity.

Plan each of your sewing projects (whether garments, accessories, or home decorating items) in advance. Where can you add ornamental details for the most artistic and pleasing results? Consider possibilities for seams and edges. Consider decorative flatlocking. What are your other options? (Fig. 1-2)

narrow
corded
edge

decorative
serged
trim

narrow
corded
edge

Fig. 1-2: *Plan your serging projects with decorative detail in mind.*

Experiment, then give it your best shot. But remember, subtlety can often be more pleasing than overdoing it, so don't try to decorate every edge or seam on any one project. Choose those areas where your ornamental serging will be the most effective.

The lessons and projects throughout this book are just a beginning. Once you understand the basics of serger sewing, you too can become a serger artist. It's simply a matter of focus and awareness. Ornamental serging can be applied to even the simplest T-shirt to make it look like designer sportswear (see page 56).

Practice, experimentation, failure, and success are all part of the process. So accept the challenge and join us in the latest phase of serger sewing—ornamental serging.

How to Use This Book

Know Your White Superlock has been designed to lead you quickly through the basics (Chapters 1 and 2) and into the fun world of ornamental serging. You'll find 38 lessons, grouped into chapters on seams, edges, trims and bindings, special techniques, serged closures, and artistic possibilities.

The lessons begin with decorative basics and progress to those requiring more advanced skill. A simple project is included at the end of every lesson so you can easily practice the techniques you have learned.

Less experienced serger users may want to follow the lessons numerically to learn basic skills before moving on to advanced ones. If you come to a term you don't understand, refer to the Glossary of Serging Terms. Experienced seamsters can easily skip around in the book, choosing to study a lesson when it applies to a current project.

Regardless of your level of experience, the Table of Contents can help you decide quickly which decorative seams, edges, bindings, or other techniques to use for a particular serger project. When you've mastered all of the lessons in *Know Your White Superlock*, you'll feel comfortable selecting even the most advanced ornamental serging applications.

Superlock Features

The *Superlock* is well designed for ornamental serging. The front and side covers on most recent *Superlock* models completely open to expose the loopers for easy threading. The open needle-plate design (with two lower cutters) allows for visibility and accuracy. All *Superlock* models use standard household needles for convenient replacement, and several models have a tension-release lever for quick changing of threads, easily removing work from under the presser foot without chaining off, and simple securing of stitching when starting or ending a seam (see page 36).

Superlock Stitch Formation

Every model of serger has one or more varying stitch options. Refer to the chart on page 8 or to your manual to determine the stitches available on your model. If this book is your own, use a highlighter pen to mark your machine's features.

4-Thread Overlock Stitch
(Fig. 1-3)

Fig. 1-3: *Stitch formation — 4-thread overlock stitch.*

■ Sometimes referred to as a 3/4-thread overlock stitch.

■ The upper looper interlocks with the left needle, so all four threads interlock.

734

734D

A White Superlock Photo Gallery

534

523

503

228

208

206

White Superlock Features

	734/734D	534	523	503
Stitch Formation:				
4-thread overlock	Yes	Yes	N/A	N/A
3-thread overlock	Yes	Yes	Yes	Yes
2-thread overedge	N/A	N/A	Yes	N/A
Number of needles	2	2	1	1
Needle type ■■	Household	Household	Household	Household
Stitch-width capacity	2 – 5mm	1.8mm or 2 – 5mm ■	2 – 5mm	2 – 5mm
Stitch-width adjustment	Remove needle	Remove needle	Change plate	Change plate
Stitch-length capacity	1 – 5mm	1 – 5mm	1 – 5mm	1 – 5mm
Stitch-length adjustment	Outside dial	Inside dial	Inside dial	Inside dial
Rolled edge	Left needle	Right or left needle depending on machine	Yes	Yes
Rolled-edge adjustment	Change plate and foot	Change plate and foot	Change plate and foot	Change plate and foot

■ A rolled edge formed with the right needle of a 2-needle model is 1.8mm wide. A left-needle rolled edge is 2.0mm wide.

■■ Organ brand "SP" needles help prevent skipped stitches on all models.

White Superlock Features

	228	208	206
Stitch Formation:			
4-thread overlock	Yes	Yes	N/A
3-thread overlock	Yes	Yes	Yes
2-thread overedge	N/A	N/A	N/A
Number of needles	2	2	1
Needle type■■	Household	Household	Household
Stitch-width capacity	1.8 – 5mm	1.8 – 5mm	2 – 4mm
Stitch-width adjustment	Remove needle	Remove needle	Change plate
Stitch-length capacity	1 – 5mm	1 – 5mm	1 – 5mm
Stitch-length adjustment	Outside dial	Outside dial	Outside dial
Rolled edge	Right needle	Right needle	Yes
Rolled-edge adjustment	Change plate and foot	Change plate and foot	Change plate and foot

White Superlock Features

	734/ 734D	534	523	503
Differential feed	734D	N/A	N/A	N/A
Tension type	Lay-in disc 1-turn (labeled and numbered)	Dial 1-3/4 rotations (numbered)	Dial 1-3/4 rotations (numbered)	Dial 1-3/4 rotations (numbered)
Thread-tension release lever	Yes	N/A	N/A	N/A
Totally visible threading	Yes	N/A	N/A	N/A
Built-in thread cutter	Yes	Yes	Yes	Yes
Elastic feet (two sizes)	Yes	Yes	Yes	Yes
Blindhem feet (two sizes)	Yes	Yes	Yes	Yes
Pearl/sequin foot	Yes	Yes	Yes	Yes
Piping foot	Yes	Yes	N/A	N/A
Owner's workbook	Yes	Yes	534 supplement	534 supplement
Instructional video	Yes	Yes	N/A	N/A

White Superlock Features

	228	208	206
Differential feed	Yes	N/A	N/A
Tension type	Lay-in disc 1-turn (labeled and numbered)	Lay-in disc 1-turn (labeled and numbered)	Lay-in disc 1-turn (labeled and numbered)
Thread-tension release lever	Yes	Yes	Yes
Totally visible threading	Yes	Yes	Yes
Built-in thread cutter	Yes	Yes	Yes
Elastic feet (two sizes)	Yes	Yes	Yes
Blindhem feet (two sizes)	Yes	Yes	Yes
Pearl/sequin foot	Yes	Yes	Yes
Piping foot	Yes	Yes	N/A
Owner's workbook	Yes	Yes	Yes
Instructional video	Yes	Yes	Yes

- Durable for seaming and decorative finishing (up to 5mm wide) and fully stretchable.

- Converts to a 3-thread overlock stitch by removing either needle. Use the left needle for a wide stitch and the right needle for a narrower stitch.

3-Thread Overlock Stitch

(Fig. 1-4)

Fig. 1-4: Stitch formation — 3-thread overlock stitch.

- Threads interlock at the seamline to form a stretchable, yet durable, seam or edge finish.

- Available on all *Superlock* models.

- Less bulky than the 4-thread stitch.

2-Thread Overedge Stitch (on the 523 model only)

(Fig. 1-5)

Fig. 1-5: Stitch formation — 2-thread overedge stitch.

- Threads do not lock at the seamline.

- Less bulky than 3- or 4-thread stitching.

- Used for decorative or lightweight edge finishing, flatlocking, or flatlock seaming. Doesn't form a (more stable) locking seam.

Superlock Feet and Accessories

All *Superlock* models have special feet and accessories to make ornamental serging easier. Refer to the *Superlock* features chart on page 8 to determine the specific options for your machine.

Standard presser foot (Fig. 1-6)— All 3/4-thread standard *Superlock* presser feet have handy cord/yarn holes to guide yarn or filler cord easily while you serge over it. The front hole

Fig. 1-6: *The standard foot on all* White Superlock *models has guides for cord or yarn built into the toe of the foot.*

guides the filler between the two needles on a 4-thread machine, while the rear hole guides it to the right of one or both needles. Refer to your manual or page 54 for complete threading instructions. The cord/yarn holes in the standard presser foot make serge-corded edges (Lesson 4), serging a fishline ruffle (Lesson 7), or gathering over filler cord (Lesson 23) especially easy.

Detachable cord guide (See Fig. 4-6, page 55)—When snapped onto the thread stand, this guide can be used to position filler cord for strengthening an edge or seam or to

create a decorative effect (Lesson 4). It is also used for filler-cord gathering (Lesson 23).

Narrow rolled-edge foot and plate (Fig. 1-7)—To serge a narrow rolled

Fig. 1-7: *The rolled-edge foot is used for the tightest narrow rolled edge.*

edge, you will need to change to a rolled-edge presser foot and plate. A narrow balanced stitch can be created with the rolled-edge plate and standard foot, but the rolled-edge foot and plate must be used to roll the edge completely.

tension-control knob

tension-control roller

Fig. 1-8: *The elastic foot guides elastic and controls the stretch with a tension-control roller.*

Elastic feet (Fig. 1-8)—An optional accessory on all *Superlock* models, these feet are available in .5mm and 1.0mm width. They guide narrow elastic and stretch it with a tension-control roller. The amount of tension can be adjusted to alter the amount of stretch. See elasticized trims (Lesson 20) and serge-shirring (Lesson 23) for applications.

Fig. 1-9: *The blindhem foot accurately guides stitching along an edge or fold—ideal for flatlocking and blind hems.*

Blindhem feet (Fig. 1-9)—These handy optional feet fit all *Superlock* models and are available in two sizes, one for light- to medium-weight fabric and one for heavy-weight fabric. In addition to blindhemming (instructions are included with the feet), they are ideal for serged tucks and for accu-

rately guiding serger stitching along a fold. For specific uses, see perfecting flatlocking (Lessons 3 and 25), serger lace (Lesson 24), and serge-picked zippers (Lesson 32).

Fig. 1-10: *The pearl/sequin foot guides trim accurately between the needle and the cutter.*

Pearl/sequin foot (Fig. 1-10)—Edges can be embellished easily using a pearl/sequin foot, available for all *Superlock* models (Lesson 28). The foot can also be used when serging over wire (Lessons 8 and 24) and for serging over trim (Lesson 27).

 Note: When using this foot, you will need to place fabric under the foot (not in the front fabric guide) in order for the needle to catch the edge or fold.

Fig. 1-11: *The piping/cording foot can be used for creating or inserting piping.*

Piping/cording foot (Fig. 1-11)— The piping/cording foot is available for two-needle *Superlock* models. It looks similar to the standard *Superlock* foot except that it has a groove on the bottom to accommodate piping. Use it to make and apply serged piping (Lesson 15) or for a double rolled edge (Lessons 5 and 19).

Snap-on guide

5-thread spool holder

Fig. 1-12: *The Super 5 Update Kit is available for the* Superlock *model 534.*

Super 5 Update Kit (Fig. 1-12)— *Superlock* model 534 can be converted to a 5-thread machine with the aid of this conversion kit. The kit has a 5-thread spool holder, enabling an extra thread spool to be positioned along-side the other four spools. An extra snap-on thread guide snaps onto the telescope guide to help direct the fifth thread. The extra thread is threaded through one of the two existing needles to create a reinforced yet stretchy seam. The Super 5 is especially helpful for a variety of decorative options—threading two decorative threads through the same needle or looper or combining a decorative thread with all-purpose thread.

Standard Superlock *accessories*—All *Superlock* sergers come with a packet of useful accessories. These are listed in your manual and include: tweezers for easy threading, an oiler and a lint brush for lint-free maintenance, spool caps, spool holders and nets for smooth feeding of thread, and a cutter replacement blade and spare needles for convenience. Also included are a needle plate and presser foot used when converting to a narrow rolled edge and screwdrivers for easier changing. Refer to your manual for detailed information.

Loving Care

Your serger is a precision instrument. If you treat it well, it will reward you with years of ornamental serging. But without proper care, it can create problems on even the simplest project.

You may not be taking your sewing machine in for regular checkups, but for your serger regular checkups are essential. The serger's timing and accuracy need to be much more finely tuned than the sewing machine's.

Follow these basic guidelines to keep your serger running smoothly: (Fig. 1-13)

After Every Project

_____ Remove the presser foot, needle plate, and needle(s).

_____ Remove **large pieces of lint** with a fluffed-out lint brush.

_____ Blow out **fine lint** with environmentally-safe pressurized air, a hair dryer, a computer vacuum, or a household vacuum on reversed air flow. OR...

_____ Use a lint brush lightly dipped in sewing machine oil to remove **fine lint** particles. The oil also provides some gentle lubrication.

N **Note:** Never blow into your serger to remove lint particles. The small amount of moisture in your breath can harm your machine.

_____ Change the needle(s).

- Use the correct type and size of needle for your fabric.

- Push the needle(s) all the way up into the needle bar.

- Be sure the long groove is still toward the front after tightening the needle-retaining screw.

■ Once a month: *Dislodge lint from tension controls.*

■ Every project: *Change needles.*

■ Once a month: *Check cutters.*

■ After every project: *Dust out lint from behind covers and under feed dogs and needle plate.*

Fig. 1-13: *Follow these basic guidelines to keep your serger running smoothly.*
■ Every 12 - 15 serging hours: *Oil as instructed in your manual.*
■ Once a year: *Take your serger to your local dealer for a checkup.*

Every 12 to 15 Hours of Serging

 Note: Oil your serger (see your manual). Use only sewing machine oil.

_____ If your serger is noisier than usual, oil it.

_____ If you haven't used your serger for several months, oil it before using it again.

_____ After oiling, test-serge on scraps of fabric to remove any residual oil.

Once a Month

_____ Remove lint lodged in the tension controls.

■ Turn the tension control to zero (or hold the tension-release lever).

■ Put knotted thread through the tension control.

■ Reset the tensions to normal (or let go of the tension-release lever) and pull the knotted thread back and forth through the controls to remove any lint.

_____ Check the cutters.

■ Do they cut ragged edges?

■ Do they have a shiny, worn look?

■ If so, replace the cutter(s) (refer to your manual for instructions or see your local dealer).

Once a Year

_____ Take your serger to your local dealer for an annual checkup.

_____ Stock up on needles, new accessories, and the latest books and information.

2. Ornamental Serging Basics

- **Tension—The Key to Success**
- **Decorative Threads**
- **Threads Other Than Decorative**
- **Shaping Materials**
- **Other Important Serging Supplies**
- **Ornamental Serging Sample Book**
- **Exploring Your Machine's Creative Limits**

Tension—The Key to Success

Once you have a thorough knowledge of serger tension adjustment, you will be able to use your machine to its fullest creative potential. On your sewing machine, you would change the tension only if there were something wrong with the stitch. *On a serger, you will need to readjust your tension settings practically every time you change your thread, fabric, or stitch type.* You'll also change tensions as you change the stitch length and width and when you want to create varied effects.

Although tension adjustment is part of any basic serger instruction, we will cover it again in this book because it is such a critical part of ornamental serging.

Changing serger tension settings is not complicated if you follow a few basic guidelines and know what a correctly adjusted stitch should look like. In a balanced 3-thread overlock stitch, the looper threads should hug the top and bottom of the fabric and overlock exactly on the edge. The needle thread should form a line along the left edge of the stitch and look like sewing machine straight-stitching on both top and bottom. (Fig. 2-1)

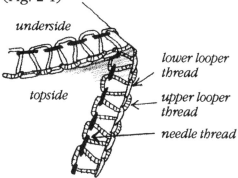

underside

lower looper thread

topside

upper looper thread

needle thread

Fig. 2-1: *When tension settings are balanced, the looper threads will hug the top and bottom of the fabric and overlock exactly on the cut edge.*

See your manual or refer back to pages 12 - 13 for examples of perfectly balanced tension for all the stitch options on your *Superlock* model.

Practicing tension adjustment

If you have never experimented with your machine's tension settings, or if you have any doubt about how to adjust the serger tension properly, try this experiment:

1. Thread your serger with different colors of all-purpose or serger thread. (For easier identification, you may want to use the same colors as those on your thread guides.) If you have a 4-thread machine, remove the left needle and test first using a 3-thread overlock stitch. Later you can convert back to 4-thread and test that as well. Adjust for a medium-length (2.5mm to 3mm), balanced stitch.

2. Find the center setting of all your tensions. Try to set the control as close to the middle setting as possible. If you tend to forget which control adjusts which looper or needle, label them with small pieces of masking tape. Study your manual and place each label on the correct control until you know it by heart. (Some models are already labeled for you.)

3. Set the lower looper tension all the way to zero. At this point, the lower looper is at the loosest tension. Leave the upper looper and needle tension on the center setting.

4. Cut two 4" by 6" rectangles from medium-weight woven fabric. Serge-seam the rectangles together along one side and examine the results. Learn what the lower looper thread looks like when the tension is at its lowest (loosest) setting. Label and save your seam sample for your sample book (see page 33).

5. Set your lower looper tension almost all the way to the highest (tightest) setting. Leave the upper looper and needle tensions at the center setting. Repeat step 4, checking the results of a tightened lower looper tension. Label and save your sample.

6. Turn the lower looper tension back to the center and loosen the upper looper tension all the way to the left. Leave the lower looper and needle tension on the center setting. Repeat step 4, checking the results of a loosened upper looper tension. Label and save your sample.

7. Repeat step 5 for the upper looper by tightening the tension and leaving the lower looper and needle tensions on the center settings.

Balancing the tension

Now you are beginning to understand the effects of changing the tension settings on your serger—and you're no longer afraid to experiment! The next step is to learn how to adjust for a balanced tension:

1. Set the tension control to the center settings.

2. Cut long 4"-wide strips from medium-weight woven fabric for testing. Put the right sides of two long strips together and serge a test seam for a few inches on the long edge.

3. Stop and look at the stitching behind the presser foot without removing the fabric. Look at the upper and lower looper threads. Remember, the looper threads should meet at the edge. If one thread is pulled *over* the edge, the other thread is too tight. First, find the one that appears to be too tight and *loosen* it. (Fig. 2-2)

upper looper too tight

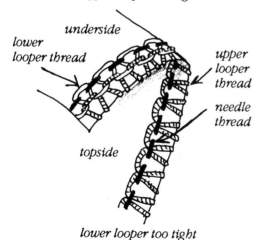

lower looper too tight

Fig. 2-2: *Find the looper tension that is too tight and loosen it.*

Serge a few more inches. If the tension hasn't been eased or is made worse, return the control to the original position and *tighten* the other looper thread (the one that appears to be too loose). Continue to test-serge and adjust—a few inches at a time—until the looper tensions are balanced.

4. Examine the needle-thread line from the right side. If it is too loose, the seamline will pull open. If it is too tight, the seamline will pucker. (Fig. 2-3) The needle thread tension won't

too loose   too tight

Fig. 2-3: *When the needle tension is too loose, the seamline will pull open. When the needle tension is too tight, the seamline will pucker.*

always need to be adjusted. Change the needle tension only if the seamline pulls open or looks puckered. Turn it to a higher number to tighten the tension or a lower number to loosen it.

Follow these guidelines to get perfectly balanced tension every time:

1. Adjust one control at a time and test-serge after each adjustment. Don't make the mistake of turning all the tension controls at the same time.

2. Make only small adjustments. A small adjustment can make a big difference.

3. When adjusting the looper tension, first loosen the looper thread that appears to be too tight. If the adjustment doesn't seem to help the problem, or if it made it worse, *put that control back where it was* and tighten the other looper tension. Continue adjusting, one control at a time (putting the setting back where you started if the change did not help), until the tension is balanced.

4. Every time you use a different type of thread or fabric, you will need to check your tension adjustments. For the most accurate adjustments, test-serge on scraps of the actual project fabric, using the same grain and the same number of layers.

Continue to practice, test, and experiment with varying fabrics and tensions. Learn to recognize what happens when you make tension adjustments. As you proceed through this book, you will find that *some very interesting novelty stitches can be formed by varying the tensions*. Both the rolled-edge stitch and flatlocking are created with tension adjustments. And that's only the beginning of a wide range of possibilities.

Confidence in using your serger and the ability to use it to its full potential come only after you are comfortable about changing tensions.

Decorative Threads

We're constantly learning about new or newly discovered threads, yarns, ribbons, and trims that can be serged ornamentally. Creative serger enthusiasts have used everything from elastic thread to fine wire to create special ornamental effects.

Many materials for decorative serging can be found in the notions and trim departments of your local fabric store. Also try sewing machine dealerships; needlecraft, yarn, and craft shops; and mail-order sources.

Follow these thread selection guidelines as a starting point to test your ornamental serging possibilities:

Puffed Serged-Braid Frogs

Thread-Chain Tassels

Double-Bound Seams

Fig. 1: *This high-fashion fall outfit is ornamented with shiny black rayon thread, serged into a decorative frog and eye-catching tassels (Chapter 8) as well as show-stopping double-bound seams (Chapter 3).*

Serge-Pleated Fabric

Decorative Exposed Seams

Serged Trim

Fig. 2: *Nubby beige fabric becomes a major fashion statement with the addition of taupe ornamental serging. Woolly nylon thread is used to ornament the collar fabric (Chapter 8), for basic decorative seams (Chapter 3), and to add serged trim to the collar edge (Chapter 5).*

Fig. 3: *Casual sportswear need not be plain. Black fringe emphasizes a yoke (Chapter 8) and coordinating serged-fold self braid (Chapter 5) adorns the neckline. A lapped and top-stitched zipper (Chapter 7) with matching fringe turns the utilitarian bag into a special creation.*

Serged-Fold Self-Braid

Thread-Chain Fringe

Lapped & Top-stitched Zipper

Serger Cutwork

Double Rolled Edge

Serged Appliqué

Fig. 4: *Crisp and fresh, this pretty dress shows off three unusual serging techniques. The bib collar is bordered with a double rolled edge (Chapter 4) and accented with serger cutwork (Chapter 8). The handbag is ornamented with coordinating serger appliqué (also Chapter 8).*

Flat-Locked Fringe

Fig. 5: *A businesslike suit is spiced up easily by adding serged piping (Chapter 5), serge-bound buttonholes (Chapter 7), and a focal-point tie with flatlocked-fringe edges (Chapter 6).*

Serged Piping

Serge-Bound Buttonholes

Elasticized Trim

Corded Flatlocking

Elasticized Binding

Fig. 6: *This solid-color swimsuit sports ornamental serging to make it anything but ordinary. Corded flatlocking (Chapter 6) highlights the trunk portion. Contrasting elasticized binding keeps the legs securely in place and elasticized trim repeats the black accent color at the neckline (both Chapter 5).*

Serged Cording

Serged Couching

Thread-Chain Cording & Tassels

Fig. 7: *Casual clothes are a perfect backdrop for ornamental serging skills. Serge-couching (Chapter 6) and matching serge-cording (Chapter 4) accent this bright red top. Serger thread-chain bracelets (Chapter 8) pull the look together.*

Balanced Decorative Edges

Serged Button Loops

Fishline Ruffles

Fig. 8: Even elegant evening wear can be enhanced with special serger techniques. Serged elastic button loops (Chapter 7), a balanced decorative edge (Chapter 4), and fluffy fishline ruffles (Chapter 6) are all featured in a coordinating metallic thread.

Decorative Serging Quick Reference Chart

USE: N - Needle
UL- Upper Looper
LL- Lower Looper
SO- Serge Over
A - All Uses

EASE:
* Easy
** Moderate
*** Challenging

TENSION ADJUSTMENT: N - None
S - Slight
L - Lots

TYPE	SIZES AND COLORS AVAILABLE	USE	EASE OF USE	TENSION ADJUST-MENT	SUB-STITUTE	DESCRIPTION	APPLICATION	NOTES
Buttonhole Twist	Variety of colors.	A	*	N-S		Slightly heavier than all-purpose thread.	Edging or flatlock seaming all type sportswear, home decorator items.	May work satisfactorily in size 14 needle, not in size 11.
Woolly Nylon	Variety, including variegated.	A	*	S		Crimped, yarn-like thread, stretchy, fluffs up when serged. May melt with hot iron.	Excellent for providing soft elastic seams on lingerie, swimwear, activewear, silky, rolled edge.	May be used through needle. Tensions may need to be adjusted. Best coverage of any lightweight decorative thread.
Rayon	Variety of colors and sizes, including new "pearl" rayon.	A	*	N-S-L (depending on size)		Shiny, silk-like thread, smooth, bright colors.	High-luster edging or flatlock seaming for elegant fashion garments and accessories.	
Silk	Variety of colors and sizes.	A	*	N-S	Rayon Threads Machine Embroidery	Shiny, soft, smooth, expensive.	High-luster edging or flatlock seaming for elegant fashion garments and accessories.	
Metallics	Variety of sizes and colors, including variegated.	A	**	S-L		Adds glitter, can be used multi-strand or combined with other threads.	Highly decorative edge for sportswear, eveningwear, holiday gifts, and home decor.	Vary greatly according to manufacturer. Avoid those with coarse, metal fibers. Experiment to find which works best.
Braids	Variety of sizes, colors and fibers.	UL, LL, SO	** to ***	L		Purchase by the yard.	Edging or flatlock, seaming of garments, accessories, home decorator, and nusery items.	Require testing and experimentation to achieve tension balance. It may be necessary to bypass tension disc altogether. Use in loopers only.

	Description	Machine Position	Rating	Weight	Thread Type	Characteristics	Uses	Notes
Ribbon	Variety of colors, fibers, including silk, acrylic, polyester 1/16 – 1/4" wide.	UL, LL, SO	***	L	Braided Rayon Ribbon	Soft knitting ribbon, bright colors.	Edging or flatlock, seaming of garments, accessories, home decorator, and nusery items.	Require testing and experimentation to achieve tension balance. It may be necessary to bypass tension disc altogether. Use in loopers only.
Braided Rayon Ribbon (Ribbon Floss)	Variety of colors, including metallic 1/8" wide.	UL, LL, SO	**	L		Soft, knitting ribbon, bright color, crosswound on tube.	Edging or flatlock, seaming of garments, accessories, home decorator, and nusery items.	Require testing and experimentation to achieve tension balance. It may be necessary to bypass tension disc altogether. Use in loopers only.
Crochet Thread	Variety of colors, including variegated and metallic.	UL, LL, SO	** to ***	L		Available in acrylic and cotton, strong thread.	Edging or flatlock, seaming of garments, accessories, home decorator, and nusery items.	Require testing and experimentation to achieve tension balance. It may be necessary to bypass tension disc altogether. Use in loopers only.
Pearl Cotton	Variety of colors and sizes—#5 and 8 are most common.	UL, LL, SO	#8 ** #5 ***	L	Crochet thread Rayon "pearl"	Soft, shiny, tightly twisted strong thread.	Edging or flatlock, seaming of garments, accessories, home decorator, and nusery items.	Require testing and experimentation to achieve tension balance. It may be necessary to bypass tension disc altogether. Use in loopers only.
Yarns	Variety of colors Two- or three-ply, Baby or Sport yarn.	UL, LL, SO	*** (Two-ply easiest)	L	Pearl cotton Woolly stretch nylon	Soft, smooth, tightly twisted.	Edging or flatlock, seaming of garments, accessories, home decorator, and nusery items.	Require testing and experimentation to achieve tension balance. It may be necessary to bypass tension disc altogether. Use in loopers only.
Monofilament Nylon	Very fine Clear or smoke color. Variety of weights— #60 and #80 (finer) are common.	N, UL, LL (Use finer weights for needle.)	*	N		Strong, invisible thread, used with decorative thread, may melt with hot iron. The higher the number, the finer the thread.	Fashion accessories, home decorator items requiring strong seams, thread invisibility.	Some brands are too heavy and wiry to loop well. Look for lightweight, supple selection.
Elastic	Various sizes, including 1/4 – 3/8" widths.	A SO-1/4" & 3/8" widths	*	S		Adds stability and can create fabric.		
Machine Embroidery Lingerie	Variety of colors.	N, UL	**	N-S		Lightweight, smooth, delicate.	Lingerie, lightweight fabrics where stress is not a factor, edging soft fabrics.	

Special Tip: Decorative threads crosswound on top-feeding cones are the easiest to use. (Fig. 2-4) Those wound in

easiest

most difficult

Fig. 2-4: *Crosswound decorative thread is easiest to use. Balls and skeins are more difficult.*

balls or skeins or sold by the yard are more difficult because they require extra care in order to help them feed evenly when serging.

Not all decorative threads will serge successfully in every machine. It's important always to test first. Allow at least seven yards for each looper you'll be testing and two yards for each needle. When estimating actual project yardage required, you will need 10 times the finished decorative serging length for each looper.

Serging decorative threads

You have three options when serging decorative threads: threading through the loopers, threading through the needle, or serging over the ornamental thread.

Most often the decorative thread is threaded through the upper looper. This part of the stitch shows on the top side as you are serging. On a rolled edge (page 58) or reversible-edge binding (page 69), the upper looper should be the only thread visible on either side.

If you want a balanced stitch (identical on both top and bottom), you will also need to thread the lower looper with decorative thread. In some cases, when the thread is not strong, the lower looper will not be able to handle a thread that works in the upper looper. This is because the upper looper thread has less movement in the thread guides and a shorter distance between the spool and the presser foot, so less stress is put on the thread.

The loopers don't pass through the fabric, so they both have larger eyes than a serger needle. This makes it possible to use thicker thread or yarn in your loopers. Consider these questions in determining whether a thread or yarn will work in the serger loopers:

1. When folded over double-layer, will the decorative thread easily pass through the looper eye? (Fig. 2-5)

Fig. 2-5: Be sure your decorative thread or yarn will easily pass through the looper eye when it is doubled.

2. Is the thread flexible enough to form a uniform stitch without catching in the loopers?

3. Is the thread smooth or tightly twisted enough to ensure trouble-free feeding and prevent fraying or snagging?

4. Is the thread yardage continuous and long enough to complete the project? (Always allow an extra 8 to 10 yards for testing.)

Some lightweight threads also fit through the needle eye. Woolly nylon, fine metallic thread, lightweight monofilament nylon, and top-stitching thread are examples. These threads therefore can be used for the ladder side of flatlocking (see page 48) or for other stitches that require loosened needle tension. In many cases,

though, you will not need decorative thread in the needle, so use all-purpose or serger thread.

If a yarn, ribbon, or trim is too heavy or wide to fit through a looper or needle, you have the option of serging over it. To do this, make sure that the stitch you use is wide enough to cover the trim without stitching into it. You also have the option of using a 3-thread balanced, rolled-edge, or flatlock stitch, so test first for the best results.

When serging over a narrow trim, insert the trim under the back of the presser foot and over the front. Make sure the trim fits to the right of the needle and to the left of the cutter. If the trim is thin enough, thread it through one of the holes in the standard presser foot. For either method,

Fig. 2-6: Serge over trim for 1" to 2" before inserting the fabric.

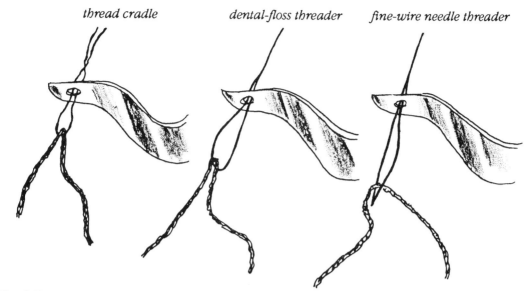

thread cradle *dental-floss threader* *fine-wire needle threader*

Fig. 2-7: *Here are options for easily threading heavy or limp decorative threads through looper eyes.*

turn the handwheel to form 1" to 2" of stitches over the trim before inserting the fabric. (Fig. 2-6, page 26) Always serge slowly. To highlight the trim rather than the stitching, use mono-filament nylon or matching light-weight serger thread in the upper looper.

If the trim is bulky, use the pearl/sequin foot or remove the presser foot and guide the trim manually between the needle and the cutter. Hold both the trim and the fabric taut. As we discuss corded edgings and other techniques requiring serging over threads or strands, we'll give more specific instructions for successful results.

Special threading tips

To begin, clip the thread you are using above the spool and tie on the decorative thread. Bypass the tension control to prevent the knot from breaking or untying as it is pulled through. Pull the knot through the remaining thread guides. You may have to clip the knot at the eye of the looper or needle and thread it through manually.

Heavy or limp decorative threads are difficult to thread through the looper eyes. Serger pros use several tricks to do the job easily. Naomi makes a thread cradle by looping a strand of all-purpose thread around the specialty thread and then threads the ends of the all-purpose thread through the eye. (Fig. 2-7) Tammy uses a dental-floss threader (available at any drugstore) for the same purpose. Fine-wire needle threaders are also available from sewing retailers and mail-order sources to simplify the threading process.

Rethread the tension control and start serging with wide, long stitches. Gradually test and alter the stitch for the desired effect. For the most accurate results, always test on scraps of actual project fabric.

Turn the handwheel a few stitches to make sure the stitches are forming correctly. Then serge slowly for a few inches before stopping to adjust the tension. One general rule to keep in mind: the more resistance a thread has, the less tension it needs to have exerted on it. For example, a rough metallic thread needs less (looser) tension and a smooth, shiny rayon needs more tension.

If the tension is too tight after adjusting it all the way, check to be sure the thread isn't hanging up on a thread guide. If it is still too tight, remove the thread from the tension control or the pincher guide. For lay-in tension discs, place a strip of transparent tape over the tension slot to keep the thread out. (Fig. 2-8)

Fig. 2-8: For lay-in tension discs, if tension is too tight, place transparent tape over the slot to keep the thread out.

On models with tension dials, if the tension is too loose at the lowest adjustment, try wrapping the thread around the tension dial twice. (Fig. 2-9)

for less tension   *for more tension*

Fig. 2-9: On models with tension dials, if the dial cannot be adjusted further, remove the thread for less tension or wrap it a second time for more tension.

Special Tip: Tensions and stitch length can vary from machine to machine, even on the same model. Your dealer cannot expand the range but can adjust the ranges slightly in one direction or the other.

Adjust to the desired stitch length. Most decorative seams and edges are serged with a satin stitch length. There should be enough thread coverage so little, if any, fabric shows through the serging. If you adjust the serger for too short a stitch length, though, the fabric may jam under the presser foot or the seam may pucker.

The thickness of the thread and the type of fabric you use will determine how short a stitch length you need. Finer thread requires a shorter stitch length for maximum coverage, while heavier thread looks better with a slightly longer stitch length. (Fig. 2-10)

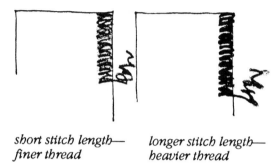

short stitch length—
finer thread

longer stitch length—
heavier thread

Fig. 2-10: *For maximum coverage, use a shorter stitch length when using finer thread. Lengthen the stitch slightly for heavier thread.*

When shortening the stitch length, you will also need to tighten both looper tensions or the stitching will hang off the edge of the fabric. (Fig. 2-11)

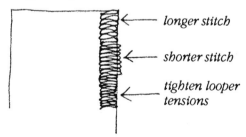

←— *longer stitch*

←— *shorter stitch*

←— *tighten looper tensions*

Fig. 2-11: *Tighten both looper tensions when shortening the stitch so stitches won't hang off edge.*

Because decorative stitching is an important part of the design of a garment or project, the stitches must be smooth and uniform. The slightest pulling of the decorative thread can narrow the stitch or even break the strand. (Fig. 2-12)

If uneven stitches are a problem, check for anything that may be causing uneven feeding of your decorative

Fig. 2-12: *Stitches will narrow or break if the decorative thread does not feed evenly.*

thread. One common problem is that the thread catches on the spool itself (prevented by using a spool cap) or winds around the spool pin under the spool. Make sure the thread is feeding evenly off the spool.

Use thread nets to control feeding of slippery or wiry thread. For threads wound on balls or skeins, rewind the thread loosely by hand onto empty cones or spools. Rewind thread and yarn quickly with a cone-winder, sold in knitting shops.

Some serger pros prefer simply reeling off several yards at a time from the ball or skein while serging. With this method, be sure that the feeding is not impeded by sewing tools cluttering your work area.

To illustrate how important even feeding can be, our serging friend Sue Green tells an amusing story. As she was working with decorative yarn in her upper looper, she kept getting uneven stitches (which she calls hiccups) in her serging. After checking all the usual trouble spots, she discovered that her kitten was playing with the ball of yarn on the floor. Even though she was pulling off the yarn as she serged, the kitten's extra pulling occasionally caused just enough tension change to create major glitches in her otherwise perfect decorative stitching.

Combining thread types

You may need to make additional tension adjustments when you are combining different thread types and using them in the same looper simultaneously. We do this for special decorative effects, such as adding a shiny fine metallic thread to woolly nylon or for toning down the color blocking of a variegated thread using one solid-color thread or another strand of the same thread with the colors aligned differently. Another thread commonly combined with a decorative one is fine elastic thread, because it adds stretch-prevention to serged edges and seams.

When combining thread types, make sure both are feeding evenly without restrictions. You may need to adjust the tension or remove one of the threads from the tension control. Always test first before serging your actual project.

Pressing over decorative thread

Some types of decorative thread (such as woolly nylon, monofilament nylon, and pearl cotton) are sensitive to a hot iron. For best results, use a press cloth to prevent melting or a permanent shine on your thread. (Fig. 2-13) Consider the fiber content of the thread and treat it similarly to a fabric of the same type. If in doubt, test first.

Fig. 2-13: *Use a press cloth to prevent melting or shine with sensitive decorative thread.*

Threads Other Than Decorative

All-purpose or serger thread: All-purpose thread is most often cotton-covered polyester, wound parallel on conventional spools. Serger thread usually has the same fiber content but is a little lighter in weight than all-purpose thread. It is crosswound on cones or tubes so that it will feed more evenly, in an upward direction, during higher-speed serger sewing.

Monofilament nylon thread:
Used for many serger techniques, this handy thread comes in either clear or smoke shades. We prefer the lighter-weight size 80 thread for use in either the needle or loopers. Monofilament nylon is practically invisible for covering serger-applied trims and for "floating" stitches on top of the fabric. Because the nylon also is strong, you can use it in the lower looper for tightening down a rolled edge or for perfecting other techniques. Be careful to prevent melting this thread when pressing.

Fusible thread: A special thread combined with a heat-activated component, this exciting new product bonds easily at the touch of a steam iron (much like fusible interfacing). Fusible thread helps stabilize and position edges and seam allowances in a wide variety of decorative techniques. We also use it to position serged braid or cord for couching and monogramming. Always test your application first on your project fabric.

Although top-stitching may be added for extra security, the pliable fusible thread bond withstands both washing and dry cleaning. For maximum fusing coverage, we usually use it in the lower looper of a 3- or 4-thread serged stitch or in the needle of a 2-thread overedge stitch. The more fusible thread exposed, the better the bond. When you use this thread in the lower looper, tighten the tension slightly so the thread does not extend past the edge of the fabric.

Always press from the top side of the stitching. Never allow the iron to touch the fusible thread directly. Because the fusible component has a low melting point, press-baste first with a warm iron. Then permanently bond using as much steam and heat as your fabric will tolerate. Allow the bond to cool before moving the fabric. Also, quickly secure seam ends with a shot of steam applied over (but not touching) the thread chain.

Shaping Materials

Clear elastic: About one-third the thickness of regular elastic, clear polyurethane elastic does not "grow" as it is stitched through. It is also impervious to nicks from serger cutters. Handy for many sewing and serging projects, it comes in five widths—1/8", 1/4", 3/8", 1/2", and 3/4".

Elastic thread: Available in a range of colors and sizes (from light-weight to cording), elastic thread has several interesting serger applications. All but the heaviest weights can be threaded through the loopers (see Lesson 34, Serged Elastic Button Loops, page 147). Elastic thread can also be serged over to create shirring or to stabilize an edge.

Fishline: If you don't already have some on hand, fishline is available at most sporting goods, discount, and drug stores. We use it for decoratively ruffling edges. Choose the clear line to avoid show-through in your project. Fishline weights vary from

12 lb. to 40 lb. Use the 12 lb. for lightweight fabrics and a heavier weight for heavier fabrics, when serging over two layers, or for extra body.

Fine wire: Wire, used to shape ornamental edges, is available in any craft store. Fine, lightweight floral wire is usually precut to 18" lengths. For projects that require longer lengths, try beading wire, which comes on spools and in a variety of colors and weights.

Batting: Various weights of batting are available in both cotton and polyester. We prefer either bonded batting, which holds together well, or fleece, which is a little thinner.

Fiberfill: This shredded batting is most often polyester and is used to stuff pillows and craft projects.

Other Important Serging Supplies

■ Your *Superlock* serger

■ Your owner's manual and all machine attachments and accessories (including tweezers and screwdrivers)

■ A straight-stitch sewing machine, preferably with zigzag capability

■ Needle-nosed pliers or needle inserter

■ Extra needles

■ Extra cutter blade (one comes with your serger)

■ Fine-wire needle threader or dental-floss threader

■ Thread nets (some are included with your machine)

■ Spool caps

■ Seam sealant like *Fray Check*

■ Washable glue stick or fabric glue (such as Aileen's *OK to Wash-It* or Magic American's *Fabric Mender Magic*)

■ Fusible transfer web (such as *Wonder-Under*)

■ Stabilizers—both water-soluble (such as *Solvy* or *Wash-Away*) and tear-away

■ Dressmaker shears

■ Rotary cutter and mat

■ Seam ripper

■ Yardstick

■ Tape measure

■ Water-soluble and air-erasable marking pens

■ Machine lint brush or canned air

■ Loop turner, darning needle, or crochet hook

■ Any other favorite sewing supplies

Fig. 2-14: Keep a sample book of notes, test results, and creative ideas.

Ornamental Serging Sample Book

We recommend that you keep a sample book of all your lesson results and other testing for later reference. One perfect way to do this is to use a *Superlock* "Owner's Workbook" (available for all models) and add extra pages for additional samples. (Fig. 2-14) Or use a standard 3-ring binder with heavy paper to mount your finished samples.

Be sure to note your tension, stitch width, and stitch-length settings for each type of stitch, thread, and fabric used. This information will be handy as a starting point for your future projects.

Put creative ideas in your sample book, too. Clip magazine photos, write notes about techniques to try, and add special instructions that come with new types of thread or other ornamental serging supplies. Refer to your sample book for inspiration and information while planning and completing each new serger project.

Exploring Your Machine's Creative Limits

As you work through this book, you will no doubt come up with bright ideas of your own. Because serger sewing is a relatively new art, there are lots of techniques and ideas yet to be discovered and developed.

Be open to experimentation. Test new serger techniques. Check our newsletter for the latest techniques. Think about how you can adapt them for your own use. Then take time to answer the following questions in order to inspire your creative efforts:

1. *How can I adapt new sewing products and threads for serger use?* With so many recent technical advances, new serging possibilities abound. Fusible thread (page 31) opened up a wealth of new techniques for us. Clear elastic and elastic thread (page 31) add even more options. Interesting new decorative threads (page 31) continue to be introduced.

2. *How can I combine craft products and ideas with my serging skills?* Many of our latest techniques and projects have come from using craft items such as fine wire (Lesson 8), water-soluble stabilizer (Lesson 37), and beads (Lesson 28).

3. *Can I convert sewing techniques for the serger in order to speed up a project or make it more durable?* Fishline ruffles (Lesson 7), lettuced edges (Lesson 5), and French seams (Lesson 1) are a breeze with the help of a serger.

4. *Are there unique stitch configurations on the serger that I can use for unusual ornamental effects?* Serger lace (Lesson 24), reversible-edge binding (lesson 9), and serger chain art (Lesson 35) were all developed because of the machine's unique stitching capabilities.

5. *Is there another way to manipulate an edge or a fold to get a different result?* Double-bound seams (Lesson 2) and edges (Lesson 14) and double rolled edges (Lessons 5 and 19) are some recent options.

6. *Can I copy a trim or decorative effect from ready-to-wear?* Look in stores, magazines, and catalogs for inspiration. Check out crafts projects, too.

The more you use your serger and experiment with all its ornamental options, the easier you will find it is to be creative and to develop ideas of your own. So start now to explore all the possibilities and really use your *Superlock* to its creative limits.

3. Decorative Seams

- **Lesson 1. Basic Seams**
- **Lesson 2. Serge-bound Seams**
- **Lesson 3. Flatlocked Seams**

Serging seams is one of the most basic uses for your serger. The type of fabric, the amount of stress placed on the seam during wearing, and personal preference are all factors in deciding on which seam to use.

Any seam may be hidden on the inside or used ornamentally, exposed on the right side of the fabric. Exposed seams are especially popular on many of today's sportier ready-to-wear garments.

When seams are exposed, they become a decorative design element. Therefore, it is important that the tension and stitches are perfect, no matter what kind of thread you use. Always test first with two layers of the project fabric and the same thread you will be using. Compare your samples with the illustrations of perfect stitch formation in your manual or on pages 5 and 12 and adjust accordingly.

When serging decorative seams, the method you used to secure seam ends is important. When a seam will be crossed by another serged seam, we usually don't secure the ends by any other method. The serged thread chains hold the ends in place until they can be seamed across and se-

cured. If additional reinforcement is needed, we straight-stitch along the needleline of the second seam for about 2" to 3" across the first seam. (Fig. 3-1)

Fig. 3-1: *Serged seams are often secured by another seam. Straight-stitching can add reinforcement.*

When the seam ends will not be crossed and secured with another serged seam, we must secure them with another method. The deciding factor is usually how much the method of securing will show. Because exposed seams are on the outside of the fabric and not worn next to the skin, our first choice is to use a drop of seam sealant on the ends. Be sure to let the sealant dry thoroughly before cutting the chain.

Special Tip: If the wet seam sealant accidentally touches another part of the project, leaving a stain, rub the spot with a cotton swab soaked in rubbing alcohol. The stain will disappear.

On *Superlock* models with tension-release levers, White educators have developed a quick method for securing seam ends. Serge a few stitches and, with the needle(s) up, press the tension release and bring the first stitch back in front of the needle(s). Then serge over the previous stitches to anchor them. Continue serging to the end of the seam. Press the tension release and position the seam back a few stitches. Reserge the last few stitches to secure the end. (Fig. 3-2)

Fig. 3-2: *Use the tension release to secure the seam ends. Serge a small section, release the tension, reposition the needle, and serge again. Repeat at the other end of the seam.*

Lesson 1.
Basic Seams

When seaming, it is important to serge-trim some of the fabric, even if it is just enough to neaten the edges. This ensures even stitching, neater edges, and better control of the width trimmed. It is easiest to trim between 1/8" and 3/8".

A basic seam can be serged with either a 3- or 4-thread stitch. The 2-thread overedge stitch will form a *flatlocked* seam (see page 47), but will not form a basic *locking* seam. If the seam will not be top- or edge-stitched but you want the seam to be as secure as possible, use a 4-thread stitch or straight-stitch along the needleline after serging a 3-thread seam.

Basic decorative seam

To serge a decorative, exposed seam, place the fabric wrong sides together and serge with the needle on the seamline. (When using two needles, the left needle will be on the seamline.) Both sides of the seam will show, so use the same type of thread in both the upper and lower loopers. You may decide to use the same color for both loopers or to vary the colors to achieve a desired effect. Depending on the seam placement, you may not need to press (see our Double-Bow Pillow project, page 40).

Create safelocked seams by pressing exposed seams to one side and top-stitching for neatness or to add strength. In this case, only the seam's upper looper thread will show. Apply top-stitching right next to the overlocked edge using a long stitch length. For more accuracy, use the blindhem foot on your sewing machine to guide your stitching evenly. Adjust the foot so the overlocked edge is next to the guide. (Fig. 3-3)

Fig. 3-3: Use a sewing machine blindhem foot to top-stitch the decorative seam to one side.

To secure an exposed seam quickly, put fusible thread (see page 31) in the lower looper when serging the seam. Before serging, determine to which side the seam will be pressed and serge with that side down. Tighten the lower looper tension slightly so the fusible thread does not show from the right side. Serge-seam. Carefully press-baste the seam to the side, then steam thoroughly to permanently fuse. For most seams, no other securing is needed.

Hidden Lapped Serging Technique

We often need to lap decorative stitching—when completing a circle, joining the ends of an opening, or (occasionally) correcting irregular areas of serging. This technique eliminates the need to serge on and off the fabric, which provides a neater (almost invisible) decorative finish.

1. Raise the needle(s) and presser foot. Then, disengage the stitches from the stitch finger. If available on your machine, press the tension-release lever to allow easy removal of the thread from the stitch finger.

2. Insert your fabric, positioning the needle(s) on the seamline. If you are joining ends of an opening or correcting irregular serging, position the needle(s) about 1/2" before the end of one side of the opening. (Fig. 3-4)

Fig. 3-4: Position the needle(s) 1/2" before the end of the serging.

3. Serge until you reach the opposite end of the decorative stitching.

4. Overlap the stitches for 1/2", being careful not to cut the original stitching with your cutters.

5. Raise the presser foot and needle(s), press the tension-release lever or manually clear the stitch finger, and pull the fabric just behind the needle(s). (Fig. 3-5)

Fig. 3-5: Raise the needle(s) and presser foot and pull the fabric behind the needle(s).

6. Serge off to form a thread chain.

7. If you're using a heavy decorative thread, dab on a drop of seam sealant and trim the chain when dry. If you're using a satin stitch and a lighter-weight decorative thread (such as

woolly nylon), lapping the stitches should secure them adequately. Simply trim away the excess thread chain after lapping the stitches.

If you are lapping decorative serging and plan to trim the edge, trim away a 2" section of the seam allowance to the serger cutting line where you plan to begin your serging. (Fig. 3-6) Then position the cutting line against the blade before starting.

Fig. 3-6: When trimming the edge, cut away 2" to position the knife on the cutting line.

Basic seam for reversibles

Basic exposed seams can also be used for two-layer reversible garments, leaving exposed decorative seams on one side and a seamline on the other. Sandwich the fabric of the seamline side (right sides together) inside the fabric of the exposed-seam side (right sides out). The wrong sides of the two fabrics will be together. Serge-seam. Open the layers and top-stitch the seam allowances to one side. (Fig. 3-7)

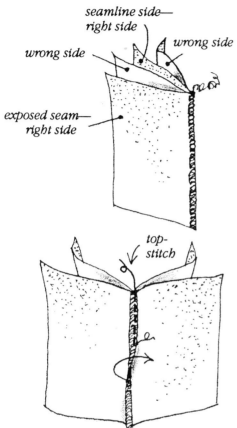

Fig. 3-7: *Sandwich the fabric layers for reversible garments. One side of the seam will have a seamline. The other side will have an exposed and top-stitched decorative seam.*

Lapped seam

A lapped seam is formed by serge-finishing the edges of both layers of fabric separately, then top-stitching one to the other. Serge-finish both layers with the needle on the

seamline. Overlap the edges, matching the seamlines. Top-stitch on the needleline, then top-stitch along the opposite side of the seam if desired. (Fig. 3-8)

Fig. 3-8: *For a lapped seam, serge-finish both edges. Top-stitch them together along the needleline. Top-stitch again on the edge if desired.*

Lapped seams are flat and very durable and are also used for reversibles. The upper looper thread on the top fabric layer is the only exposed part of the seam. For reversibles, both layers are serge-finished with one upper looper thread exposed on each side of the garment and top-stitched on the matched needlelines only.

Decorative French seam

Serged French seams on the outside of a garment or project form a decorative detail resembling a tuck. With the fabric right sides together, serge a narrow- to medium-width (2-2.8mm), medium-length, 3-thread seam. Fold the wrong sides of the fabric over the seam and press carefully. Straight-stitch next to the cut edges, enclosing the seam. Use your sewing machine's blindhem foot to sew a perfectly even width, placing the fold of the seam next to the guide on the foot. This ornamental French seam works best on straight seams. (Fig. 3-9)

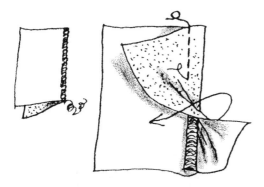

Fig. 3-9: *For an exposed French seam, serge a narrow seam with the right sides together. Wrap the fabric to enclose the serging and straight-stitch.*

Mock flat-felled seam

The mock flat-felled seam, simple yet durable, is used on heavy fabrics. Top-stitching with decorative thread adds ornamental interest to your finished project. Right sides together, straight-stitch the seam with a 5/8" seam allowance. Serge-finish the edges together and press them to one side. For extra strength, use fusible thread in the lower looper when serge-finishing and fuse the allowances to one side. From the right side, top-stitch over the allowances right next to the seamline and again 1/4" away. Use a long stitch length and a decorative thread like buttonhole twist.

Project: Double-Bow Pillow

Exposed satin-stitched seams become a decorative detail on this attention-getting pillow. It's simple to serge and requires only 3/4 yard of fabric. (Fig. 3-10)

Fig. 3-10: *This double-bow pillow features decorative seams-out detail.*

Foot: Standard
Plate: Standard
Stitch: 3- or 4-thread overlock
Stitch length: Satin
Stitch width: Wide (4mm or 5mm)
Thread: Contrasting color to fabric
  Needle(s): All-purpose or serger thread
  Upper looper: Decorative or all-purpose thread
  Lower looper: Decorative or all-purpose thread
Tension: Balanced
Needle(s): Size 11/75
Fabric: 3/4 yard 45"-wide solid or print cotton chintz
Notions: Polyester fiberfill

1. Cut two 14" by 20" rectangles, two 12" by 16" rectangles, and one 6-1/2" by 12" rectangle.

2. Adjust your serger for a satin-length, 3- or 4-thread overlock stitch. (Fig. 3-11)

Fig. 3-11: A satin-length overlock stitch forms a pretty, textured seam.

3. Raise the needle(s) and presser foot and clear the stitch finger manually or use the tension-release lever. Place the two large rectangles wrong sides together. Insert the fabric under the presser foot, positioning the needle(s) on the seamline 2" past the center of one long side (see the hidden lapped serging technique, page 37). Serge-seam, barely trimming the four edges to neaten. Serge on and off at the corners and end the stitching about 5" from the beginning serging. Lightly stuff the pillow with fiberfill and serge-seam the opening closed using the hidden lapped serging technique.

4. Repeat step 3 for the two smaller rectangles.

5. Fold the remaining rectangle in half lengthwise with the wrong sides together. Using a longer (3mm) stitch length, serge-seam the long edge. Refold with the seam in the center of the strip and serge-finish both ends.

6. Center the smaller pillow section over the larger one. With the seam underneath, wrap the serged strip from step 5 around the center of both pillows to form a tie. Hand-tack the strip on the back side of the pillow to secure.

Lesson 2. Serge-bound Seams

One of the first things we learn about the serger is that it neatly finishes seams by overlocking the edges. Developing this feature further, we can vary stitch length, width, and thread used to decoratively serge-finish seam allowances. We can also use the serger to speedily encase seam allowances in binding fabric.

Decorative serge-bound seams can be so attractive that we often choose to feature them on the outside of a project. This works especially well for jackets and coats because the seam allowance is featured ornamentally on the outside, while the inside shows only a neat seamline.

A professional-looking binding must be a consistent width. With the serger's exact cutting ability and the even width of its stitches, a consistent-width serged binding is almost foolproof.

Serged seam binding

This decorative seam finish is usually seen on the inside of unlined coats or jackets. It is easily achieved by finishing the seam-allowance edges with decorative, satin-length serging and then sewing the seam with a 5/8" seam allowance. (Fig. 3-12)

Fig. 3-12: For serged seam binding, serge-finish the allowance edges with a satin-length stitch before seaming.

If you have a 4-thread serger, remove the left needle. Put a contrasting-color or tone-on-tone decorative thread in the upper looper. Adjust for a short (1-1.5mm) stitch length and a medium to narrow stitch width. Serge-finish from the right side of the fabric, barely skimming the edge. We like to experiment with different stitch widths, depending upon the type of thread we use. Finer thread needs more coverage and looks best with a narrow stitch width. Heavier thread is often more attractive in a wider stitch. Also try woolly nylon or glossy pearl rayon thread for attractive serged seam bindings.

Serged French binding

For a couture effect, add serged French binding to seams using a contrasting or matching strip of fabric. Try combining different types and colors of fabrics for stronger emphasis. Nylon *Lycra* works well as binding fabric because it folds tightly against the seam allowance. In addition, its bright colors can add a stunning contrast to dark or basic colored fabric. Try binding velvet with satin, wool with lightweight synthetic suede, or woven fabric with knits.

1. For a finished binding width of approximately 1/4", cut a binding strip 1" wide (four times the desired finished width). The width of the finished binding should be no wider than the width of your serger's widest stitch. If the seams to be bound are straight, the strip can be cut on the crosswise grain. However, if the bound seams are even slightly curved, cut woven strips on the bias or knit strips in the direction of greater stretch (usually crossgrain).

2. Adjust for a 5mm stitch width (or the widest on your machine) and a medium stitch length. From the wrong side, with fusible thread in the lower looper, serge-finish one long binding edge, trimming a scant 1/8".

3. Because the binding strip has a narrower seam allowance, it may be easier for you also to pretrim the fabric seam allowances to 1/4". Or serge the seam and trim it before applying the binding. As you become more comfortable with the application, you'll be able to serge-seam with a full seam allowance and apply the binding simultaneously. (Fig. 3-13)

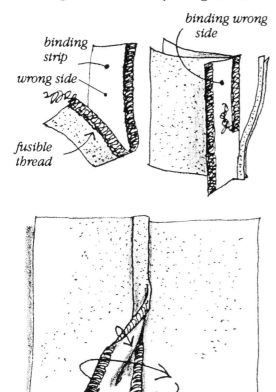

Fig. 3-13: *For serged French binding, finish the binding-strip edge with fusible thread in the lower looper. Serge-seam the binding and fabric together. Wrap the binding around the seam allowance and fuse it in place.*

This one-step method is the easiest and fastest unless the fabric is difficult to manage. If the fabric is rigid, slippery, or must be held taut while serging, straight-stitch or baste the seam first and trim the seam allowances to 1/4" before applying the binding.

Place the right sides of the fabric together, aligning the binding strip on top over the seamline, fusible side down. (To position serged French binding on the outside of your garment, place the fabric wrong sides together.) Serge-seam the unfinished edges, leaving about a 1/4" seam allowance. The needleline of the serging should be on the seamline of the project. For accuracy, especially if your widest stitch is 4mm, straight-stitch at 1/4" and serge-finish the edges together. (Serge-finishing the edges results in a smoother binding.)

If desired, you may change back to serger thread in the lower looper before serge-seaming. Do not stretch while seaming straight binding. For outer curves, ease the binding slightly, and for inner curves stretch it slightly. Wrap the binding smoothly around the seam allowance to encase it. Carefully press-baste to position the binding, then steam-press to fuse securely.

If you are applying a French binding without fusible thread, it is not necessary to serge-finish one long edge of the binding. Serge-seam the binding to the fabric, wrap the binding around the seam allowance, press, and stitch-in-the-ditch. Trim the unfinished long edge of the binding close to the stitching on the underside. Press the binding to one side and top-stitch next to the folded edge to secure. (Fig. 3-14)

Fig. 3-14: *Make a French binding without fusible thread by serge-seaming the strip to the fabric. Wrap the strip around the seam allowance and stitch-in-the-ditch. Trim the unfinished edge, then top-stitch the binding to one side.*

Double-bound seam

This self-bound seam takes some extra time and skill to construct, but it is very durable and a real show-stopper. Both seam allowances are wrapped with self fabric, then decora-tively serged from the right side. If you use a 5mm stitch width, finished

decorative seams can be almost 1/2" wide. This double-binding method will be adapted for edges and decora-tive detail in later lessons.

1. To allow the extra fabric needed for wrapping a 1/4" seam allowance, before cutting out your garment or project, add an additional 1/2" to each edge that will be bound.

2. With right sides together, straight-stitch a seam using the seam allow-ance recommended on your pattern. (The seam allowance is usually 5/8" but may be 1/2" on home decorating projects.)

3. Press the seam allowances open and trim one allowance to a scant 1/4". From the right side, wrap the fabric securely around the trimmed allowance, forming a scant 1/4" fold. Press. (Fig. 3-15)

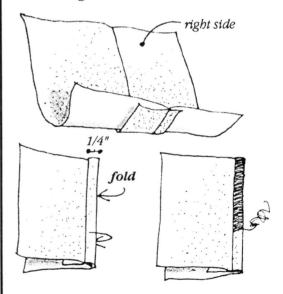

Fig. 3-15: *Make a double-bound seam by trimming the right seam allowance and wrapping the fabric around it. Serge-finish the fold.*

Special Tip: To minimize bulk on fabrics that do not ravel easily, test-trim the seam allowance to 1/8" before wrapping, then still press a scant 1/4" fold.

4. Use decorative thread in the upper and lower loopers and serger thread in the needle(s). Adjust for a wide, short (1-2mm) stitch. Use a 5mm-wide stitch for the widest possible binding (just less than 1/4" on both allowances). For a stitch width narrower than 5mm, adjust the fold width so that the serged stitch will cover the entire fold. Test first.

5. Serge along the fold from the right side of the fabric, being careful not to cut the fold. The needle (the left needle on the 4-thread overlock stitch) should be on the seamline. Adjust the tension so the overlocked stitches are tight against the fold.

6. Repeat steps 3 to 5 for the other seam allowance. When serging, make sure the needle stitches are right on or just inside the needleline of the first row of serging. (You will be serging in the direction opposite the first row of serging.) (Fig. 3-16)

7. Press the seam allowances open on the right side of the fabric. Use a press cloth, if necessary, to prevent melting the thread or leaving a shine.

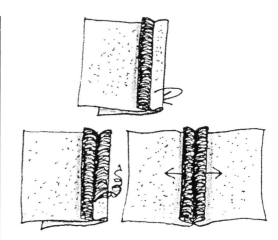

Fig. 3-16: Trim, wrap, and serge the other allowance, overlapping the needlelines. Press the allowances open.

Optional: If you will be securing the finished double-bound seam to the fabric, use decorative thread in the upper looper only. Use serger thread in the needle(s) and lower looper. Top-stitch along each side of the binding. Or you may choose to use fusible thread in the lower looper when serge-finishing the folds, so you can fuse the binding to the fabric.

Double-piped seam

For this variation of the double-bound seam, follow the same procedure but use a narrow balanced stitch on the 1/4" folds. The seam allowance will need to be trimmed to 1/4" (not narrower) so that it will catch in the narrower decorative serging and not pull out.

Note: With this technique part of the fabric will show be tween the two sides of the binding. With a narrow, balanced stitch, the needlelines will not overlap. (Fig. 3-17) Alter stitch characteristics to vary the effect.

Fig. 3-17: *The double-piped seam is a double-bound seam that is serged with a narrow, balanced stitch.*

Project: Hobo Bag

A double-bound seam is featured on this easy-to-make, versatile bag. Vary the pattern size for different uses or to suit your personal style. (Fig. 3-18)

Fig. 3-18: *This easy hobo bag features a double-bound seam.*

Foot: Standard
Plate: Standard
Stitch: 3- or 4-thread overlock stitch
Stitch length: Short (1-2mm)
Stitch width: Wide (4 or 5mm)
Thread: Contrasting color
    Needles(s): All-purpose or serger
    Upper looper: Woolly nylon
    Lower looper: Woolly nylon, serger thread, or fusible thread
Tension: Balanced
Needle(s): Size 11/75
Fabric: 3/4 yard 45"-wide water-repellent fabric or soft upholstery fabric
Notions: One pair 1" D-rings; 20" of 3/4"-wide *Velcro*; 1 yard of 1"-wide cotton or nylon strap (Fig. 3-19)

Fig. 3-19: *The hobo bag pattern grid—each square is 2".*

1. Cut two bag pieces using the pattern grid.

2. Center one piece of *Velcro* on each wrong side of the top of the bag. Adjust for a medium stitch length and width. From the right side, serge each top of the bag, catching the *Velcro* in the stitching.

Special Tips: When serging with *Velcro*, do not use woolly nylon in the looper that carries stitches onto the *Velcro* piece. The woolly nylon's crimped fibers can catch on the *Velcro*'s hooks and loops. Also test the stitch length first. You may need to lengthen the stitch when serging over *Velcro*.

3. Top-stitch the lower edge of the *Velcro* to each side of the bag.

4. With the right sides of the bag pieces together, straight-stitch around the lower edge with a 1/4" seam allowance. Trim one of the seam allowances to 1/8". Wrap the fabric around the trimmed seam allowance and press lightly (see Fig. 3-15, page 44).

5. Serge along the fold, being careful not to cut the fold.

6. Repeat steps 4 and 5 for the other seam allowance.

7. Press open the seam allowances on the outside of the bag.

Optional: To secure the seam allowances to the bag, use fusible thread in the lower looper when serge-finishing the fold. Then fuse the bound seam in place. Or top-stitch the bound seam allow-

ances to the bag.

8. Serge across both narrow ends with fusible thread in the lower looper. Wrap each end around a D-ring. Fuse and top-stitch to secure the

Fig. 3-20: *Secure the D-rings and straps by serge-finishing with fusible thread. Fuse it into position and top-stitch to reinforce it.*

D-ring. (Fig. 3-20)

9. Serge-finish each end of the strap with fusible thread in the lower looper. Insert each end of the strap through a D-ring. Fuse and top-stitch to secure.

Lesson 3. Flatlocked Seams

A flatlocked seam is always exposed on both sides of the fabric, so it can be used to add an interesting design detail. We most often see flatlocked seams on delicate lingerie and other garments on which sturdy seams are not essential. Although a flatlocked seam is relatively secure, it is not your best option for durability.

Perfecting flatlocking

The 2-thread overedge (model 523 only) and 3-thread overlock stitches are most commonly used for flatlocking. A 2-thread flatlock uses less thread and therefore makes a finer, lighter-weight, and flatter seam. For both 2-thread and 3-thread flatlocking, the needle thread tension is loosened so that it overlocks with the looper thread past the edge of the fabric. Because the needle thread is so loose, the seam can be pulled open until the stitches lie flat. (Fig. 3-21)

The perfect flatlocked seam should be pulled completely flat. To do this, you must allow the stitches to hang off the edge as you serge. Feed the fabric under the presser foot slightly away from the cutter. Your stitches will interlock beyond the edge, and you'll never have to worry about the cutters trimming your fabric. No amount of pressing will correct a flatlocked seam that cannot be pulled completely flat. Use a blindhem foot to guide the edge for an even flatlocked seam. Adjust the guide so the stitches will hang off the edge.

When flatlock seaming, you must trim the edges before serging because your fabric is fed through slightly away from the cutters so the stitches will hang off the edge. If you are flatlock seaming a loosely woven fabric that will ravel and could pull

out during use, serge-finish the cut edges first with a narrow, medium-length, balanced stitch using matching thread.

You may choose to have either the loops or the ladder side of a flatlock showing on the right side of your project (see Fig. 3-21). Both create a

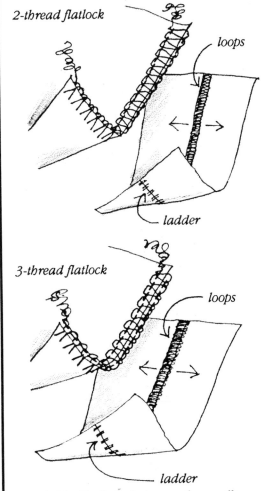

2-thread flatlock

loops

ladder

3-thread flatlock

loops

ladder

Fig. 3-21: *To flatlock, loosen the needle thread. Allow the stitches to hang off the edge. Pull the stitches flat after serging.*

distinctive design detail. When flatlocking with decorative thread, keep in mind which part of your stitch will be exposed. Seaming with right sides together, the decorative thread must go through the eye of the *needle* if you want the ladder on the outside. But if the loops will be on the outside (seaming with wrong sides together), the decorative thread must be in the *lower looper* of a 2-thread flatlock and in the *upper looper* of a 3-thread flatlock. For additional details on decorative flatlocking, see Lesson 25 (page 119).

Reinforced flatlock seaming

We often use this durable flatlocked seaming method. First straight-stitch the seam on your sewing machine. You may choose to serge-finish the edges before stitching. Fold on the seamline with the wrong sides together if you want the loops to show. Fold with right sides together if you want to feature the ladder stitches. Using your widest stitch width, flatlock over the folded seam. Pull the stitching flat. If you have not serge-finished the seam allowances, trim them close to the stitching. (Fig. 3-22)

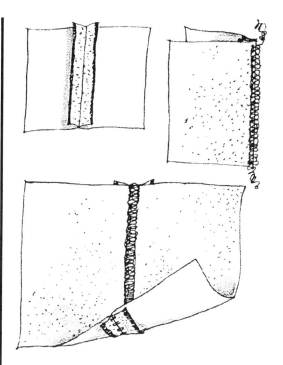

Fig. 3-22: *For reinforced flatlocking, straight-stitch the seam. Fold the fabric and flatlock over the seamline.*

 Optional: Eliminate the straight-stitching step by pressing the seam allowances back and placing them together. Flatlock over the folds and pull flat. This also makes a durable flatlocked seam.

Test each fabric or combination of fabrics before you flatlock. You may need to adjust tensions to accommodate the different thicknesses of your fabric. After flatlocking lace to tricot, for example, you may have to readjust your tensions before flatlock seaming two layers of tricot.

Project: Quick Slip

Whip up a pretty slip for any occasion with a length of tricot, two pieces of lace, and only three flatlocked seams. (Fig. 3-23)

Fig. 3-23: Use flatlock seaming to make a quick and easy slip.

Foot: Standard
Plate: Standard
Stitch: 3-thread flatlock
Stitch length: Medium to long (3 - 4mm)
Stitch width: Medium to wide (2.8 - 5mm)
Thread: Matching color
  Needle: Serger or machine embroidery
  Upper looper: Serger or machine embroidery
  Lower looper: Serger or machine embroidery
Tension: Flatlock (needle thread loosened)
Needle: New, sharp size 11/75
Fabric: 1 fabric length of nylon tricot, as long as you want your slip
Notions: Stretch lace (at least 3/4" wide, with one flat edge) to equal waist measurement; flat lace (with one flat edge) to equal slip bottom-edge measurement

1. Cut a fabric rectangle for the slip body. The length should equal the finished length desired minus the width of the flat lace. The width should be the hip measurement (measured 9" below the waist or at the widest part of the hip) plus 4". (Fig. 3-24)

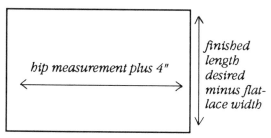

hip measurement plus 4"

finished length desired minus flat-lace width

Fig. 3-24: Cut nylon tricot for the slip.

2. You may want to serge-finish the upper and lower edges of the slip with a narrow, balanced stitch and matching thread to stabilize them and prevent them from rolling while flatlocking.

3. Adjust to a flatlock stitch. With right sides together, flatlock the flat lace to the bottom of the slip. Pull the seam flat.

4. Pull the stretch lace around your waist to a comfortable measurement (4" to 6" less than the waist measurement). Quartermark both the upper edge of the slip and the stretch lace. Match the markings. (The slip fabric is still flat, unseamed at the side.)

5. With the wrong sides together and the stretch lace on top, flatlock the stretch lace to the slip, stretching the lace to fit. Avoid hitting the pins.

6. Using the flatlock stitch and with right sides together, flatlock the side seam, matching the top and bottom laces. The less visible ladder stitches will show on the right side. Secure the seam ends by knotting the tails and trimming the remaining chain.

4. Decorative Edges

Finishing edges is a basic serger function. In fact, it is the only way some home-sewers use the serger. But edge-finishing can go way beyond the basics. By making simple tension changes and using decorative thread, you can transform edges into an ornamental element. When decoratively serge-finishing, it is important to consider how you will use the finished garment or project. If an edge will receive stress during use or wear, it must be stabilized in some way during construction or finishing. The stabilizing technique may be inconspicuous or decorative. Always test first with the thread and actual fabric you will be using.

When testing, look for stretching of the edges after they have been serge-finished. To prevent this, you may need to serge over a stabilizer such as elastic, cording, or decorative trim. Or you may choose to serge over the fold of the fabric (see pages 61 and 74). Decorative serged binding (featured in Chapter 5) will also stabilize an edge.

Check to see if the decorative serged stitch will pull away from the edge easily. (This occurs most often on chiffon and loosely woven or bias fabric.) If it does, you may need to lengthen or widen the stitch, try another kind of decorative edge, or save the fabric for another project.

Lesson 4. Balanced Decorative Edges

As soon as you've mastered tension adjustment, you're ready to embellish your garments and other projects with simple ornamental edges. If just the top edge will be exposed, use decorative thread in the upper looper only. If both sides of the serging will show, use decorative thread in both loopers. (Fig. 4-1)

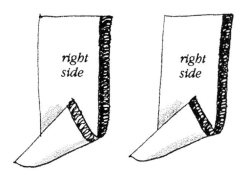

Fig. 4-1: On a balanced edge, feature decorative thread in the upper looper if only the right side will be exposed. When both sides will show, use it in both loopers.

When decoratively serging curved edges, use a medium or narrow stitch width for easier handling and a neater stitch. If you plan to trim the edge while serge-finishing, clip away 2" of the seam allowance to the serger cutting line where you plan to begin and end the serging. (See the instructions for the hidden lapped serging technique, page 37.)

When serging outside corners, we usually simply serge off the fabric at each corner and then serge back onto the adjoining side. Most often, we secure the thread chain at each corner with seam sealant and clip the tail when dry. This method eliminates any pretrimming if your project seam allowances are wider than the finished serged stitch.

Serge-scalloped edge

Your sewing machine and serger can team up to create some unusual ornamental effects. If your sewing machine has a variety of decorative stitches, try different ones in combination with a serged edge. Most sewing machines have a blindhem stitch, which can be used to add a scalloped edge to your project. In testing, we have found that this stitch works best on a folded edge or two layers of light- or medium-weight fabric.

1. Serge-finish the edge. Use the same thread in both the upper and lower looper for ease in scalloping. To begin testing, adjust for a satin stitch length. The width of the stitch and the appearance of the scallops will vary with the weight of the fabric. Use your widest 3-thread stitch for medium- to heavy-weight fabrics and a narrower width for lightweight fabrics. (Fig. 4-2)

Fig. 4-2: Use a wide stitch for medium- to heavy-weight fabrics. Use a narrower stitch for lightweight fabrics.

2. Thread your sewing machine with thread matching the serged edge and adjust it for a blindhem stitch. Set the stitch width the same or slightly narrower than the serge-finished edge. With the serging to your left and the body of the fabric to your right, blindhem stitch the edge, allowing the zigzag of the stitch to go off the edge to form a scallop. You may have to tighten the needle tension slightly to make the edge more scalloped. Adjust the stitch length to test different sizes of scallops before finishing the garment edge. (Fig. 4-3)

Fig. 4-3: *Test the length of a sewing machine blindhem stitch to create the desired size of scallop.*

S **Special Tip:** When using the blindhem stitch to scallop the edge of a project, you must feed the bulk of the fabric through the machine to the right of the needle. To avoid having to do this, use your machine's shell stitch (reversible blindhem stitch) if you have one. This will create the same stitch, but the bulk of the fabric remains to the left of the needle.

Serge-corded edge

Serging over filler cord (such as one or more strands of heavier thread, string, or cording) creates a corded overlock that can be used to stabilize a serged edge and add durability. The size of the filler cord or the number of strands used will change the thickness of the serged edge. When decorative thread and a satin stitch length are also used, the serge-corded edge becomes an attractive ornamental feature. (Fig. 4-4)

Fig. 4-4: *Serge over filler to create a corded edge.*

When serging over filler cord, it is important that the cord is guided between the needle and the cutters without stitching or cutting it and that the upper looper goes cleanly over the top of the filler. The *Superlock* presser foot is specially designed to guide filler cord into the proper position. The holes in the foot also act as a gauge to limit the size of the filler for easy passage under the upper looper.

When the filler is threaded through the front hole in the foot and serged over, it falls between the two needles (just to the right of the left needle in a wide 3-thread stitch). When the filler is threaded through the rear presser-foot hole, it falls to the right of any needle setting. (Fig. 4-5) Thread filler through both holes simultaneously (using a 4-thread stitch) for a double-corded edge.

Fig. 4-5: Thread filler through the front hole to guide between the needles, or through the rear hole to guide to the right side of the stitch.

The *Superlock* has been designed with special guides for smooth threading of filler cord. (Fig. 4-6)

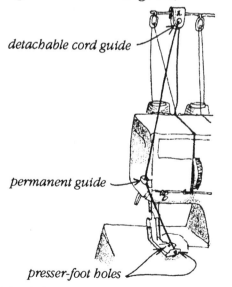

detachable cord guide

permanent guide

presser-foot holes

Fig. 4-6: Superlock system for guiding filler cord.

1. Place the filler cord behind the spool-pin base.

2. Snap the detachable cord-guide accessory onto the thread guide, as shown, and thread the filler through it.

3. Then thread the filler through the permanent cord guide on the side of the machine and through the left needle-thread guide.

4. Insert the cord down through either the front or rear presser-foot hole—the front to feed it between the two needlelines or the rear to feed to the right of any needleline.

5. Draw the filler toward the back under the remainder of the foot.

Begin serging over the filler cord by turning the hand wheel to make at least one stitch. Then begin serging at a slow speed to see that the cord is feeding correctly.

 Note: When feeding the cord through the front hole and between the two needles, you may have to hold the cord taut behind the presser foot when starting. This ensures that the filler will pass cleanly between the needles. Increase the serging speed only after properly positioning the filler.

Add durability and create a decorative edge at the same time by threading filler cord through the rear hole and serging over it with a 3-thread stitch just wider than the filler. Use monofilament nylon thread in the upper looper and a decorative filler for an interesting ornamental effect.

Use several strands of matching-color filler cord for a thick, beefy serge-corded edge. The number of strands you can use is limited to the number that will pass easily through the presser-foot holes. Adjust for a narrow, balanced stitch and a short stitch length to replicate manufactured cording.

Allow several inches of the filler to extend at the beginning and end of the serging. To stabilize the edge, or when serge-cording around a curve, pull up on the filler to ease in the serged edge. Then knot securely. But remember, the rigid filler cord eliminates any stretch of the serged stitch.

For a cording that gives with the fabric as well as stabilizes, use elastic cording or 1/8" transparent elastic for filler. The elastics are especially good for serged filler cording on sweatering, interlocks, and other knits.

Project: Sunburst T-shirt

Create a designer top by serge-decorating an inexpensive T-shirt. Have fun experimenting with different designs, thread types, and colors. (Fig. 4-7)

Foot: Standard
Plate: Standard
Stitch: 3-thread
Stitch length: Short (1 - 2mm)
Stitch width: Narrow (1.8 or 2mm)

Fig. 4-7: *Decorate a T-shirt with narrow, balanced stitching. Ruffle the seamlines by stretching as you serge.*

Thread: Contrasting color
    Needle: All-purpose or serger
    Upper looper: Woolly nylon
    Lower looper: Woolly nylon
Tension: Balanced
Needle: Size 11/75
Fabric: Oversized T-shirt
Notions: Beads (optional)

1. Purchase an inexpensive over-sized T-shirt from a discount store. Most come in packages of three at additional savings, so you won't have to make a big investment for your testing.

2. With an air-erasable marking pen, draw a simple sunburst design on the front of the T-shirt. To do this, make six lines extending 6" to 7" from the neckline seam. Two lines will begin about 3/4" on either side of the center front. Two additional lines on each side begin at the neckline approximately 1-1/2" and 3" past the first lines. (Fig. 4-8)

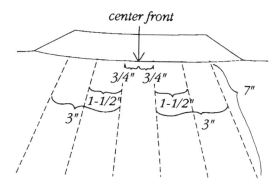

Fig. 4-8: Draw a sunburst design on the T-shirt front with an air-erasable marker.

3. With the wrong sides together, fold the T-shirt on each line. Starting at the neckline, serge over the folds to the end of marked lines. Stretch the knit to ruffle the fabric as you serge, being careful not to cut the folds with the cutters. Be sure to guide the folds so the looper threads meet exactly at the edge. (If the fold is too wide, it will stretch the thread so the thread will not have as much coverage.) Serge off the fabric at the end of each line and leave 4" to 6" of thread chain attached.

4. Using the same stitch adjustment and stretching as you sew, serge around the outer edge of the ribbed neckline. Start at one shoulder and end by serging approximately 1/2" over the beginning stitches, using the hidden lapped serging technique (page 37). Raise the presser foot and needle and pull the T-shirt away from the presser foot. Clip the thread ends.

5. Fold the ribbing to the inside along the neckline seamline. With wrong sides together and the ribbing on top, begin serging over the fold, starting at one shoulder and stretching as you serge. (Fig. 4-9) Catch the

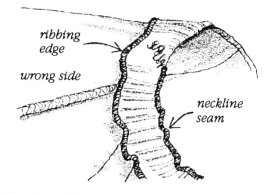

Fig. 4-9: After ruffling the ribbing edge, fold the ribbing to the inside and serge over the neckline seam.

ends of the sunburst lines in the stitching. Serge slowly when crossing the ends of the lines to allow maximum thread coverage. End by serging approximately 1/2" over the beginning stitches and pulling the top away from the presser foot as in step 4.

6. Repeat step 4 for the lower edge and sleeves. Start and end the lower-edge serging at one side seam. Start and end on the sleeves at the underarm seam.

7. For a mock band effect at the lower edge, fold back 3" and pin with wrong sides together. Serge over the fold, stretching as you sew. Repeat for the sleeve edges, folding back 1-1/2" before serge-finishing.

8. Tie on decorative beads to the end of each sunburst thread chain if desired.

Lesson 5.
Rolled Edges

The narrow rolled edge (or hem) makes a wonderful finish for most light- and medium-weight fabrics on any project from napkins to expensive dresses. With some adjustments, you also may be able to use a rolled edge on heavier fabrics. A rolled-edge finish may be either decorative or inconspicuous, depending upon the thread used. One of the original selling points of the home serger was its ability to do a rolled edge more neatly, quickly, and easily than on a sewing machine.

Consult your manual for instructions on converting to a narrow rolled hem. On some models, you will need to remove the right needle, while on others you will remove the left.

The only visible thread in a correctly adjusted 3-thread rolled edge is the upper looper thread. (Fig. 4-10) When the tension is adjusted properly, the upper looper thread is pulled entirely around the edge of the fabric from needleline to needleline. The lower looper thread is tightened and forms a line that is almost straight. Both the lower looper and needle threads can barely be seen.

For a rolled edge, you will need only one spool or cone of decorative thread. With some decorative threads

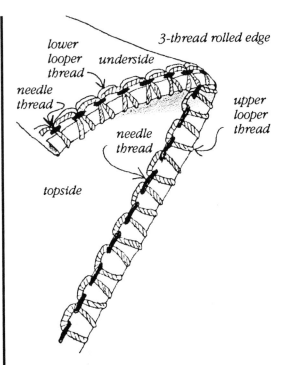

Fig. 4-10: The upper looper thread wraps the edge. The lower looper and needle threads are barely visible.

(and on certain fabrics), you may find it impossible to wrap the upper looper thread on a 3-thread rolled edge entirely around to the back using tension adjustment alone. One example is slick rayon thread. Use woolly nylon or monofilament nylon thread in the lower looper. The added strength of the nylon will help roll the edge completely. With monofilament nylon in the lower looper, loosen the tension before starting to serge. If the tension is too tight, the monofilament thread may snap. Because it is practically invisible, monofilament is more difficult to rethread.

To form a rolled-edge stitch, the fabric must roll completely around the needlelike stitch finger. When this doesn't happen, short threads may poke out through the stitching. (Fig. 4-11) Try these solutions to eliminate the problem:

Fig. 4-11: Threads may poke through the stitching on a rolled edge if the seam allowance is not wide enough to wrap to the underside or if the stitch is too long.

1. Shorten the stitch length to completely cover the edge with serged stitches.

2. Use monofilament or woolly nylon thread in the lower looper.

3. Place a strip of water-soluble stabilizer over the fabric edge before rolling it. Tear away the excess stabilizer after serging.

4. Press 1/4" to the wrong side and serge the rolled edge over the fold (see Serge-a-fold, page 61).

N **Note:** On some models, slightly widening the bite of the stitch is another way to eliminate threads that poke through a rolled edge. Check your manual or see your dealer to learn whether the

cutter can be moved on your machine and how to do it properly. We find it easier to begin serging a rolled edge with the cutter set for a wide bite. Then we adjust by moving the cutter toward the presser foot if threads extend beyond the stitching on the underside. (Fig. 4-12)

Fig. 4-12: Adjust the cutter for a narrower bite if threads extend beyond the stitching on the underside.

Wiry fibers in your fabric or serging on the crosswise grain may also cause threads to poke through, but these problems are usually corrected by making these adjustments.

When serging loosely woven or lightweight fabrics, the rolled edge may pull away from the fabric. This occurs most often when serging with a short stitch length. If this happens, lengthen the stitch slightly. You may have to widen the bite, if possible. The grainline of the fabric may also be a factor when the edge separates from the fabric. Test-serge on both the lengthwise and crosswise grains, as well as on the bias.

Lettucing

Lettucing the edge is a finish used only on fabric that will stretch, such as on knits and bias wovens. To make a ruffled lettuce edge, you must stretch while serging using a very short (satin) stitch length. (Fig. 4-13) Be

Fig. 4-13: Lettuce the edge of a stretch or bias fabric by stretching while serging.

careful not to bend the needle while stretching the fabric. If you have differential feed, adjust it to 0.7 to help with the stretching.

Because the fabric is stretched while serging, you may need to widen the bite, if possible, to allow enough fabric to roll over the stitch finger.

Double rolled edge

Two rows of rolled edge serged directly next to each other make an unusual ornamental detail that is also very durable. Use two contrasting thread colors, or try two different thread types for a heightened effect.

1. Serge the wrong side of one edge of the fabric with a satin rolled edge, leaving several inches of thread chain. Woolly nylon or a heavier rayon will provide the maximum thread coverage. (Fig. 4-14)

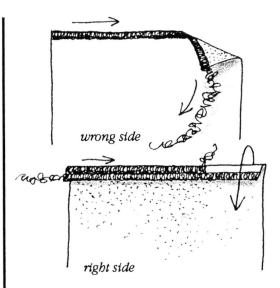

wrong side

right side

Fig. 4-14: Create a double rolled edge by serging one row from the wrong side. Then fold the stitching to the right side and serge the second row on the fold.

2. Rethread the upper looper with a contrasting thread.

3. With right sides together, refold the fabric next to the first rolled edge, leaving just enough width for another rolled-edge seam allowance.

4. Holding the thread chain to prevent jamming, serge a second rolled edge over the fold with the needle right next to the needleline of the original stitching. For serging accuracy, line up the first rolled edge with the raised ridge on top of the rolled-edge presser foot. (Fig. 4-15) You will be serging in the opposite direction from the first serging.

Fig. 4-15: Use the ridge on the presser foot as a guide for the second row of the double rolled edge.

S **Special Tip:** For ease in serging a double rolled edge, use the piping foot (see page 15) while serging the row. (Fig. 4-16) You'll have a small gap between the two rolled edges, but they will be perfectly even.

groove
piping foot

Fig. 4-16: Use the piping foot for a perfectly even double rolled edge.

5. Carefully press the double rolled edge flat.

Scalloped rolled edge

The scalloped rolled edge is similar to the scalloped edge made using balanced stitching (page 53). This edge finish is seen on the finest ready-to-wear lingerie. If you are using a scalloped rolled edge on nylon tricot, remember that tricot rolls to the right side. For the nicest rolled edge and the least frustration, serge the rolled edge from the wrong side.

Serge-a-fold

The rolled edge is a durable edge in itself. But if you prefer more body on the edge, are having trouble with threads poking through the stitching, or feel the serged edge may pull off a loosely woven fabric, press the edge 1/4" to the wrong side and serge the rolled edge over the fold. (Fig. 4-17) On the wrong side, trim the raw edge right next to the serging.

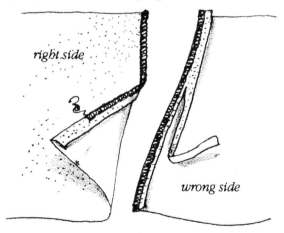

right side

wrong side

Fig. 4-17: For durability and to eliminate threads poking through the stitching, serge over a folded edge. Trim the excess seam allowance on the wrong side.

For even more durability, combine serging on the fold with scalloped edging. If you are using a scalloped rolled edge on a single knit, the decorative stitch has a tendency to roll to the right side. To prevent this and add more body, serge-finish the edge with a narrow, balanced stitch, press 1/4" to the wrong side, and serge over the fold. Finish with the blindhem stitch to create scallops.

Project: Christmas Tree Bags

These cute little Christmas tree bags are quick to make for gifts or decorating. The rolled-edge stitch seams and finishes the bags in one step, leaving attractive thread chains for the handles. (Fig. 4-18)

Fig. 4-18: *Stow tiny gifts, candies, or holiday ornaments in these simple little tree bags. The rolled-edge seams and handles are serged all in one.*

Foot: Rolled edge
Plate: Rolled edge
Stitch: 3-thread
Stitch length: Short (rolled edge setting on 1)
Stitch width: Narrow (to roll the edge)
Thread: Contrasting color
  Needle: All-purpose or serger
  Upper looper: Heavier metallic thread, like *Candlelight*
  Lower looper: Monofilament nylon
Tension: Rolled edge
Needle: Size 11/75
Fabric: Scraps of Christmas fabric
Notions: 4 bells for each bag

1. Cut two 2-1/2" by 3" rectangles for each bag. With a cup or jar lid, round the two lower corners of each rectangle. (Fig. 4-19)

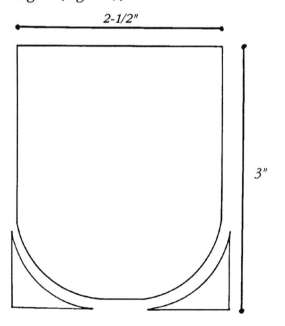

Fig. 4-19: *Cut two rectangles 2-1/2" by 3". Round the lower corners.*

2. Cut a side and bottom strip 8" long by 1-1/2" wide for each bag.

3. On the top of each rectangle and the short end of each strip, fold 1/4" to the wrong side and serge over the fold. Trim the fabric close to the stitching on the wrong side.

4. Serge the strip around the sides and bottom of one rectangle, with wrong sides together and the rectangle on the top. (Fig. 4-20) Leave about 6" of thread chain on each end.

Fig. 4-20: Leaving a long thread chain, serge the side strip to the bag piece. Pull the strip around to meet curved edges.

Hold the thread chain taut to prevent jamming. When serging the curves, pull the straight edge of the strip around to meet the curved edges.

5. Repeat step 4 for the other rectangle.

6. Tie a bell to the end of each chain and knot the four chains together about 2" from the bells (see Fig. 4-18, page 62).

Lesson 6.
Picot Edges

The picot edge is a version of the rolled edge and is most often used on soft fabric such as tricot. It finishes edges of lingerie garments and silky scarves beautifully. Simply alter a rolled-edge stitch (see page 58) for a long stitch length and a slightly tightened upper looper tension to make an attractive picot edge. (Fig. 4-21)

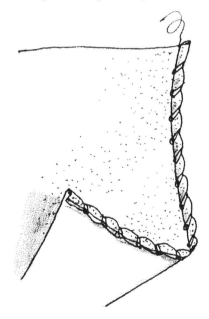

Fig. 4-21: A picot edge is serged by lengthening and slightly tightening the upper looper of a rolled-edge stitch.

Project: Pocket Scarf

A scrap of silky fabric and a simple picot-rolled edge combine to make this pretty pocket accessory. (Fig. 4-22)

Fig. 4-22: A picot-edge pocket square is a simple serged project.

Foot: Rolled edge
Plate: Rolled edge
Stitch: 3-thread
Stitch length: Long (4 - 5mm)
Stitch width: Narrow (1.8mm or
    2mm)
Thread: Matching color
    Needle: All-purpose or serger
    Upper looper: Medium-weight
        rayon thread
    Lower looper: All-purpose or
        serger
Tension: Narrow rolled edge with
    upper looper tension tightened
Needle: Size 11/75
Fabric: 8" by 8" square silk or silky

1. Begin at one corner. Raise the presser foot and needle. Insert the fabric against the cutters and just under the needle. Make two stitches by hand, turning the wheel to anchor the needle into the fabric.

2. Begin serging, holding the chain taut behind the presser foot and the fabric taut in front of it. Just skim the edge of the fabric with the cutters. Serge off the opposite end.

3. Repeat steps 1 and 2 for the other three corners.

4. Secure the corners with seam sealant and clip the threads when dry. Tuck the scarf into a pocket.

Lesson 7. Fishline Ruffles

The beautiful fishline ruffle, like its ready-to-wear forerunner, is most often seen on special-occasion garments and floral-like embellishments. Fishline is applied to the edge of the fabric similarly to filler cord, using a short- to medium-length rolled-edge stitch. (Fig. 4-23)

Fig. 4-23: Fishline ruffles are used for unusual ornamental effects.

Fishline is available at most sporting goods, discount, and drug stores in weights varying from 12 lb. to 40 lb. The lighter weight is better for lightweight fabrics like tulle and netting. Use a medium weight (25 lb.) for fabrics such as satin and taffeta. Also use a heavier fishline if you are serging over two layers of fabric or if you want extra body. If you are edge-finishing a lightweight or sheer fabric such as tulle, be sure to use clear fishline.

Serging on bias fabric creates the prettiest ruffles, but on a loosely woven fabric the stitching may pull off. As an alternative, cut the fabric on the lengthwise grain.

While serging, it is important to guide accurately and **serge slowly**. If you accidentally cut the fishline while serging over it, you will need to rework part of your project.

For the tightest fishline edge, use the rolled edge foot and plate. Place the fishline under the back of the presser foot and hold it against the ledge on the top of the foot to guide it between the needle and the cutter. For easier fishline application (but a looser rolled edge), use the standard presser foot instead, along with the

rolled-edge plate. Insert the fishline through either the front presser-foot hole (for a left-needle rolled edge) or rear hole (for a right-needle or single-needle rolled edge) to guide it accurately.

When serging over fishline, leave a long tail at the beginning and end of the serging (about half the ruffle length). First serge over the fishline for several inches, then place the fabric underneath. Do not stretch while serging. (Fig. 4-24) After serging, stretch for the amount of ruffling or flouncing desired.

Fig. 4-24: *For fishline ruffles, serge over fishline, then stretch after serging.*

Project: Ruffled Doily

A fishline ruffle adorns the edge of this charming doily. Use it under a dining table centerpiece or to add a decorative touch on a small table or chest. (Fig. 4-25)

Fig. 4-25: Fishline ruffles edge a centerpiece doily.

Foot: Standard for serge-finishing; rolled edge for ruffle
Plate: Standard for serge-finishing; rolled edge for ruffle
Stitch: 3-thread balanced for serge-finishing; 3-thread rolled edge for ruffle
Stitch length: Medium (3mm) for serge-finishing; short (1mm) for rolled edge
Stitch width: Wide (4mm or 5mm) for serge-finishing; narrow (1.8mm or 2mm) for rolled edge
Thread: Matching color
  Needle: All-purpose or serger
  Upper looper: All-purpose or serger for serge-finishing; rayon for rolled edge
  Lower looper: All-purpose or serger for serge-finishing; monofilament nylon for rolled edge
Needle: Size 11/75
Fabric: 1/4 yard polyester/cotton eyelet; 1 yard matching woven cotton
Notions: 4 yards clear 30-lb. fishline; contrasting-color buttonhole twist or crochet thread for gathering

1. Cut a 9" circle from the eyelet, using a plate or lid as a pattern. Serge-finish the edge.

2. Cut 4"-wide bias strips from the matching woven cotton and serge-seam them to make 2 yards of ruffled trim.

3. Change to the rolled-edge foot and plate. With rayon thread in the upper looper and monofilament nylon thread in the lower looper, serge-finish one long edge of the trim with a rolled edge.

4. Change to the standard foot and thread fishline through the front presser foot hole and under the back of the foot. Serge over approximately 6" of fishline before inserting the fabric under the presser foot. Serge-finish the other long trim edge over the fishline, leaving approximately 6" of fishline at the end. After serging, stretch the fishline edge to ruffle.

5. Gather the ruffle on the edge opposite the fishline 3/8" from the rolled edge. Zigzag over a strand of buttonhole twist or crochet thread, being careful not catch the heavier thread in the stitching. Position the left side of the presser foot next to the rolled edge as a guide.

6. Gather the trim to fit the outer serge-finished edge of the eyelet. Straight-stitch the two short ends of the trim to form a circle. Use a short stitch length to secure the fishline.

7. Distribute the gathers evenly and top-stitch the trim to the eyelet circle by zigzagging over the gathering line. Be careful not to catch the heavier gathering thread in the stitching. Remove the gathering thread to complete the doily.

Lesson 8.
Wire-shaped Edges

Much like fishline, fine wire can be used to shape serged edges. Unlike fishline, however, it is rigid and can be formed into almost any shape. (Fig. 4-26)

Fig. 4-26: *Fine wire shapes a delicate rolled edge.*

Fine wire is available in any craft store. We first used lightweight floral wire to shape edges of serged flowers and for serged-wire ornaments. Be-

cause most floral wire is precut to 18" lengths, we also now use fine beading wire, which comes on spools and in a variety of weights and colors.

When you serge a wire-shaped edge, it is essential that you guide the wire carefully and **serge slowly**. If you serge too fast, you may hit the wire with a needle, which could throw your serger out of alignment. Wire-shaped projects are for more experienced serger users, and even they need to be very careful.

For the most common application of a wire-shaped edge, use the rolled-edge foot and plate. Guide the wire under the back of the presser foot and between the foot and the cutter in the front. Hold the wire against the side of the foot in front, as shown, to keep it away from the cutter. (Fig. 4-27)

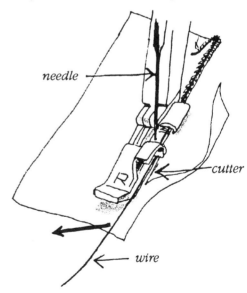

Fig. 4-27: *When serging over fine wire, hold it against the side of the foot to prevent cutting it.*

Another method of applying a wire-shaped edge is to use the pearl/sequin foot (see page 14) and the rolled-edge plate. Although the edge will not roll as tightly, the foot extensions guide the wire safely between the needle and cutter.

When serging over wire, leave at least a 1" tail at both ends for securing. Begin by serging over the wire for at least one additional inch. Pull gently on the thread chain and the wire tail to guide the serging smoothly. Then raise the presser foot and position the fabric under the foot and wire. Serge slowly. After some fabric clears the back of the presser foot, bend the wire back over the fabric to anchor it during the remainder of the serging. (Fig. 4-28)

Fig. 4-28: Start serging over wire, then insert fabric. Bend the wire back over the fabric to anchor.

Project: Wind Twister

This colorful outdoor ornament is shaped by rolled-edge serging over wire on one long edge. It twists merrily as the breezes blow. (Fig. 4-29)

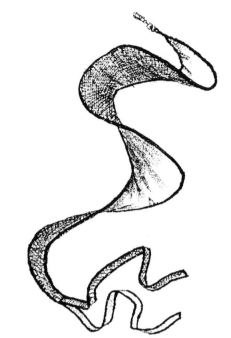

Fig. 4-29: Wind twister with wire-shaped edges.

Foot: Rolled edge; pearl/sequin foot for wire application
Plate: Rolled edge
Stitch: 3-thread
Stitch length: Short (1mm)
Stitch width: Narrow (1.8mm or 2mm)
Thread: Coordinating color
   Needle: All-purpose or serger
   Upper looper: Woolly nylon
   Lower looper: Woolly nylon
Tension: Rolled edge
Needle: Size 11/75
Fabric: 1/2 yard each of two colors 45"-wide water-repellent nylon, such as taffeta or *Ripstop*
Notions: 20-gauge beading wire (found in craft stores), one barrel swivel (from fishing supply stores)

1. Using the pattern grid (Fig. 4-30), cut one twister and one 18" by 2" strip from each piece of nylon.

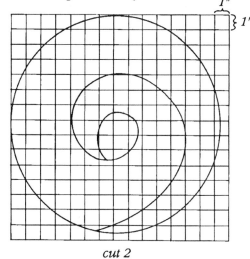

cut 2

Fig. 4-30: *Pattern grid for wind twister.*

2. Adjust for a rolled edge. Serge-finish the two long sides and one short end of each strip.

3. Serge the matching color strip to the narrow end of each nylon twister piece, right sides together.

4. Place the twister pieces wrong sides together and serge-finish the inner side of the circle.

5. Serge over 4" to 5" of wire, then insert the top of the twister and serge the wire to the outer edge of the twister circle, stopping approximately 1" past the tail seamline. Then serge off the fabric but continue serging over the wire for another 6". Raise the presser foot and the needle, pull the wire back and away from the presser foot, and serge off. Cut the wire, leaving 12" past the end of the serging.

6. Smooth the fabric over the wire, beginning at the upper edge. Twist the lower end of the wire back on itself to secure, and clip away the excess wire. Attach the barrel swivel to the serged wire at the top of the twister.

7. Place the twister on a flat surface and flatten the wire into the original circle shape. Hang the twister from the barrel swivel.

Lesson 9. Reversible-edge Binding Stitch

The upper looper thread wraps the fabric edge to form the reversible-edge binding stitch. A medium-width stitch works best for this edge finish because it allows the thread to cover the edge entirely. Similar to the rolled-edge stitch, reversible-edge binding is used on heavier fabrics so the edge does not roll under. Single-layer coats and blanket edges are common applications. Use heavier thread in the upper looper for a more durable edge.

Reversible-edge binding is formed by loosening the upper looper tension and tightening the lower looper tension. The thread should completely wrap the edge and look the same on both the upper and under side. (Fig. 4-31, page 70) If the thread does not wrap completely after loosening the tension, try taking it out of the first thread guide below the ten-

Fig. 4-31: *For reversible-edge binding, loosen the upper looper and tighten the lower looper. The upper looper thread should completely wrap the edge.*

upper
looper
thread

sion control. If additional loosening is needed, take the thread entirely out of the tension control. On models with lay-in discs, place a strip of transparent tape across the top of the machine to prevent the thread from slipping into the tension guide.

 Special Tip: If tension adjustments give a less-than-perfect stitch, switch to woolly nylon in the lower looper. This strong thread often helps to wrap the stitch completely.

The reversible-edge binding stitch is a simple but decorative edge finish, ideal for place mats, potholders, or cozies made from quilted fabrics. Before serging the edge of quilted fabric, compress the thickness by zigzagging over the seamline with a long, wide stitch. Then serge directly over the zigzagging.

Project: Wool Lap Robe

The top of this 48" by 72" lap robe can be crazy-quilted from serged-together wool scraps. Or choose a soft wool yardage to complement your decor. (Fig. 4-32)

Fig. 4-32: *Wool lap robe combines wool scraps with a flannel backing. The edge is finished with a reversible-edge binding stitch.*

Foot: Standard
Plate: Standard
Stitch: 3-thread for decorative edge; 3- or 4-thread for serging patchwork
Stitch length: Short (1.5 - 2mm) for binding; medium for serging patchwork
Stitch width: Narrow to medium (1.8 - 3.5mm) for binding; wide (4mm or 5mm) for serging patchwork
Thread: Contrasting or matching color
Needle(s): All-purpose or serger
Upper looper: Acrylic or cotton crochet thread for binding; serger thread for patchwork

Fig. 4-33: *Serge together wool scraps for top of lap robe.*

Lower looper: All-purpose, serger, or woolly nylon
Tension: Tighten the lower looper and loosen the upper looper for the binding; balanced for serging patchwork
Needle(s): Size 14/90
Fabric: Wool scraps to make a 48" by 72" piece (or 2 yards of 54" or wider soft wool or acrylic) for the robe top; 2 yards of 54" or wider flannel for the backing

1. If you are using wool scraps, serge them together in any pattern to construct a piece measuring 48" by 72". (Fig. 4-33, page 71) Or cut the lap robe top from soft wool or acrylic to the same measurement. Cut a flannel backing piece measuring 48" by 72".

2. Adjust for a reversible-edge binding stitch.

3. With the wrong sides of the top and the backing together, serge both lengthwise edges. Then serge the crosswise edges.

4. Secure the thread chain on each corner by threading it back through the binding stitch using a darning needle or a loop turner.

Lesson 10. Reversible Needle-wrap Stitch

Another decorative reversible stitch is the needle wrap, also called the blanket stitch. In this crochet-like edging, the needle thread wraps to the edge on both sides of the fabric, so the decorative thread used must be able to be threaded through the needle. The looper threads interlock at the edge of the fabric. (Fig. 4-34) Use the needle-wrap stitch as a decorative detail on an already-finished edge (such as a faced neckline or a hem foldline), or use it to finish edges on firmly woven fabric.

Fig. 4-34: The reversible needle-wrap stitch makes a crochet-like edging. It is formed when the needle tensions are loosened and the looper tensions are tightened.

Use a medium- or wide-width 3-thread overlock stitch for this edging. Loosen the needle tension and tighten the upper and lower looper tensions so the threads interlock on the edge. If the threads do not overlock exactly at the edge, adjust them slightly with your tweezers.

If you cannot loosen the needle thread entirely to the edge by making a tension adjustment, use a medium stitch width instead of the wider 4mm or 5mm width. Try woolly nylon in the loopers to help perfect this decorative stitch, or remove the thread from the first thread guide.

The look of a crocheted edge is most easily created by using a long stitch length for the needle-wrap stitch. It also works best with the heaviest possible thread that can fit through the needle eye.

Project:
Quick Potholder

Whip up a batch of simple washable potholders with reversible needle-wrap edging. You will always have clean ones on hand, and they're great for gifts, too. (Fig. 4-35)

Fig. 4-35: *Speedy serged potholders are made by sandwiching insulating material between quilted fabric, then needle-wrapping the edges.*

Foot: Standard
Plate: Standard
Stitch: 3-thread
Stitch length: Medium (3mm)
Stitch width: Medium to wide (2.8 - 5mm)
Thread: Contrasting color
    Needle: Buttonhole twist
    Upper looper: Woolly nylon

Lower looper: Woolly nylon
Tension: Loosen the needle tension and tighten the looper(s) tension
Needle: Size 11/75 or 14/90
Fabric: 1/4 yard single-faced quilted; 1/4 yard insulating material, like *Thinsulate* or a *Teflon* ironing-board cover

1. Cut two 8" by 8" squares of the quilted fabric and one of the insulating fabric for each potholder.

2. Layer the quilted fabric with wrong sides together and sandwich the insulating fabric in between.

3. Round the corners using a small bowl or lid as a guide.

4. Zigzag around the edges to compress the quilted fabric.

5. Adjust your serger for a reversible needle-wrap stitch. Test on project scraps following the instructions on page 72.

6. Starting in the middle of one straight side, serge around the edges using the needle-wrap stitch and just skimming the edges with the cutters. Overlap the beginning stitching for about 1/2". Then raise the presser foot and needle and pull the potholder away from the foot. Dab the ends with seam sealant and clip the tails when dry.

7. After serging, you may have to pull the needle thread slightly with tweezers, especially on the corners, so the overlocking looper thread is right on the edge.

8. Hand-tack a round plastic curtain loop to one corner if desired.

5. Decorative Trims and Bindings

Decorative trims and bindings can be serged directly onto the edge of your fabric, creating self-binding for craft and home decoration projects, as well as for garments from sporty to elegant. Trims and bindings can also be produced using a separate strip of fabric, which is then attached to your garment or project.

Many of the edge finishes you learned in Chapter 4 can be used separately or in combination to make a wide variety of ornamental trims and bindings. In addition to adding a unique decorative element, trims and bindings also help finish and stabilize project edges.

When applying edge-finishing or self binding directly to your fabric, always test first for stretching. If the area you will be finishing (especially a bias-woven or a cross-grain knit edge) stretches during the application, serge your trim onto a strip of fabric and bind the edge instead.

Lesson 11. Serged-fold Self-Braid

Many pretty edge finishes are not as stable as we may need for a particular project or fabric. In many cases, a neckline that is finished single-layer will stretch out. Or a single-layer sleeve edge on a loosely woven fabric may not hold up. With serged-fold self-braid, the fabric edge is folded for more durability before serge-finishing. Heavy threads serged on the fold of heavy fabric can look similar to an actual braid trim. Lighter-weight threads serged on the fold of fine fabric give a more delicate, but stable, finish.

1. Press 1/2" to the wrong side. Turning less than a 1/2" allowance may be more difficult to keep a uniform edge.

2. Top-stitch 1/8" from the fold with a long stitch length. If your finished project edge will be visible from both sides, trim the allowance close to the top-stitching.

3. Put decorative thread in the upper looper and, if the underside will be seen, also use decorative thread in the lower looper. If only the right side will be exposed, you may use all-purpose or serger thread in the lower looper as well as in the needle.

4. Place the folded edge next to the cutter and serge with a short, narrow, and balanced 3-thread stitch. Guide carefully or use a blindhem foot to prevent cutting the fold (see page 14).

 Special Tips: If you are using heavy thread, lengthen the stitch to prevent jamming when you begin to serge. Too much thread coverage may also cause stretching or ruffling of the edge. If your model has differential feed, set it on 1.5 to ease in the edge (especially on bias edges). Always test first on project fabric scraps.

Fig. 5-1: Create serged-fold self-braid by pressing 1/2" to the wrong side and serge-finishing the fold. Trim the allowance to the stitching before serging if the wrong side will be visible; do this after serging if it will not.

5. If you haven't previously trimmed the excess allowance, do so now. Use sharp embroidery or appliqué scissors and trim close to the serging. (Fig. 5-1)

To vary the serged-fold edge, adjust for a rolled-edge stitch (page 58) or a reversible-edge binding stitch (page 69).

For a more pronounced serged-fold self-braid, serge over filler cord as discussed in Lesson 4 (page 54). (Fig. 5-2) For bias and curved areas, pull on the filler to ease the serged edge.

right side

Fig. 5-2: Serge over filler threads for more pronounced braid.

Project: Lace-edged Handkerchief

Glossy serged-fold self-braid and dainty lace finish the edge of this feminine handkerchief. Make four out of only one-third yard of fabric. (Fig. 5-3)

Fig. 5-3: Lace-edged handkerchief with serged-fold braid edging.

Foot: Standard or blindhem
Plate: Standard
Stitch: 3-thread
Stitch length: Short (1-2mm)
Stitch width: Medium (2.8mm or 3.5mm)
Thread: Matching color
  Needle: All-purpose or serger
  Upper looper: Rayon
  Lower looper: All-purpose or serger
Tension: Balanced
Needle: Size 11/75
Fabric: 1/3 yard organdy or fine batiste
Notions: 1-1/4 yard 1/2"- to 1"-wide flat scalloped lace (with one straight edge) for each handkerchief

1. Cut an 11" by 11" square of fabric.

2. On two opposite edges, press 1/2" to the wrong side.

3. Top-stitch 1/8" from the fold. Trim the allowance close to the stitching.

4. Serge-finish both folds with a medium, balanced 3-thread stitch.

 Optional: Use the blindhem foot as a guide for even stitching on all models. On 4-thread models, use the left needle only.

5. Repeat steps 2, 3, and 4 for both remaining edges.

6. Fold 1/2" of the lace to the wrong side at one end. Beginning 1" from one corner, lap the serge-finished handkerchief edge over the straight edge of the lace with the right sides up. Top-stitch along the edge of the serged-fold self-braid, close to the needleline, catching the lace in the stitching.

7. Fold the lace at each corner to miter. When you reach the beginning of the lace trim, fold 1/2" to the right side and lap it 1/2" under the beginning lace before completing the top-stitching. (Fig. 5-4)

Fig. 5-4: Lap folded ends of the lace to finish handkerchief.

Lesson 12. Quick-fused Self-Braid

Another simple self-trim is created by serge-finishing garment or project edges from the wrong side using fusible thread in the lower looper. The serged edge is then folded to the right side and fused into position.

The width of the finish can vary by pressing additional fabric plus the serged edge to the right side. For this variation, the wrong side of the fabric will show as part of the braid. Therefore, the wrong side of the fabric must match or intentionally contrast with the right side.

1. Thread your serger with decorative thread in the upper looper, fusible thread in the lower looper, and all-purpose or serger thread in the needle.

2. From the wrong side, serge-finish the edge with a short, wide, and balanced 3-thread stitch.

3. Press the edge to the right side and fuse in place. If you are pressing more than the width of the serged stitch to the right side, cut out the project with a corresponding allowance for the extra fabric. (Fig. 5-5)

Fig. 5-5: For thread-fused self-braid, decoratively finish the edge from the wrong side with fusible thread in the lower looper. Press the stitching to the right side and fuse it next to the edge or further over.

For a heavier braid, add a wide decorative finish over a narrow self-braid.

1. Serge-finish the edge from the wrong side with a narrow, medium-length, and balanced 3-thread stitch with fusible thread in the lower looper.

2. Fold the stitched edge to the right side and fuse to secure.

3. Change to decorative thread in the lower looper and adjust your serger for a wide satin stitch. Serge over the narrow fused edge. (Fig. 5-6)

Fig. 5-6: For heavier braid, make a narrow thread-fused self-braid. Then serge over it with decorative thread and a wide stitch.

Project: Quickie Shoe Bags

The casing for these fast and easy shoe bags is decoratively finished with quick-fused self-braid. The flannel fabric serves a double purpose: It keeps the shoes clean and buffs them at the same time—great for a business traveler. (Fig. 5-7)

Fig. 5-7: Flannel shoe bags feature an easy thread-fused self-braid casing.

Foot: Standard
Plate: Standard
Stitch: 3-thread
Stitch length: Short (2mm) for decorative; medium (2.5-3mm) for serge-finishing
Stitch width: Wide (4mm or 5mm)
Thread: Contrasting color for decorative; matching for serge-finishing
Needle: All-purpose or serger
Upper looper: Crochet thread for decorative; all-purpose or serger for serge-finishing
Lower looper: Fusible thread for decorative; all-purpose or serger for serge-finishing
Tension: Balanced
Needle: Size 11/75
Fabric: 1/2 yard cotton flannel
Notions: 1 pair 27" shoelaces

1. For a pair of shoe bags, cut two 15" by 17" rectangles from the flannel.

2. From the wrong side, decoratively serge-finish one 15" edge on each piece for the upper casings (using crochet thread in the upper looper and fusible thread in the lower looper).

3. Rethread the upper and lower loopers with all-purpose or serger thread. Serge-finish the remaining three sides of both pieces.

4. Fold each bag lengthwise, right sides together, and straight-stitch the lower edge with a 1/4" seam allowance. Pivot at the corner and continue straight-stitching the side seam, ending 1" from the top edge. Back-stitch to secure the stitching. (Fig. 5-8)

Fig. 5-8: Straight-stitch the bottom and side of the bag, leaving 1" unstitched at the top edge.

5. On each bag, fold the decoratively serged edge 1" to the right side and carefully press to fuse the casing edge. Top-stitch over the serged needleline to secure. Insert a shoelace into the casing and draw the bag closed.

Lesson 13.
Serged Self-Binding

A simple self-binding technique uses part of the fabric to bind the edge. It is stable as well as decorative, and can be a good option for a neckline facing or a center-front band. Self-binding is most often used on straight edges and stable woven fabrics, but it can be applied to curved areas on knit fabrics as well.

The width of the finished binding is determined by the width of the serged stitch. Use the widest stitch width possible on your serger. The 5mm stitch (available on most *Superlock* models) with heavy-weight decorative thread makes the beefiest self-bound edge.

To make serged self-binding, add a 7/8" binding allowance to the pattern edge. Use a heavy decorative thread in the upper looper and all-purpose or serger thread in the needle(s) and lower looper.

1. With the wrong side up, serge-finish the edge.

2. Fold the serged edge 7/8" to the wrong side.

3. Rethread the upper looper with serger thread. From the wrong side of the garment, serge along the fold without cutting it. If the width of your stitch is narrower than 1/4", straight-stitch 1/4" from the serged edge. (Fig. 5-9)

wrong side

decorative thread

top-stitching

right side

Fig. 5-9: *Fold the decorative edge to the wrong side and serge over the fold. Fold the edge back to the right side and top-stitch.*

4. Fold the decoratively serged edge to the right side (encasing the serged fold) and top-stitch to secure.

Optional: Use fusible thread in the lower looper to add even more stability and eliminate the final top-stitching. Fuse to secure instead.

Project: Canvas Tote Bag

Serged self-binding stabilizes and decoratively finishes the top of this easy-to-make tote. A 42" length of 36"-wide or wider fabric makes two bags. (Fig. 5-10)

Fig. 5-10: *This canvas tote bag sports serged self-binding and webbing straps.*

Foot: Standard
Plate: Standard
Stitch: 3- or 4-thread
Stitch length: Short (1-2mm) for
    decorative; medium for serge-
    seaming
Stitch width: Widest
Thread: Contrasting color for
    decorative; matching for serge-
    seaming
    Needle(s): All-purpose or
        serger
    Upper looper: Cotton crochet
        thread for decorative; all-
        purpose or serger for serging
        fold and seaming
    Lower looper: All-purpose or
        serger (fusible thread optional)
Tension: Balanced
Needle(s): Size 14/90
Fabric: 1-1/6 yards heavy cotton
    canvas or cotton duck
Notions: 3 yards of 1"-wide cotton
    webbing (if you want straps long
    enough to fit over your shoulder,
    you will need 3-3/4 yards)

1. Fold an 18" by 42" rectangle from the fabric.

2. Apply serged self-braid to the two short ends of the rectangle.

3. Fold the webbing into two equal lengths for the straps.

4. Fold 1-2" to the wrong side on each end of both straps. Place the straps on the right side of the bag piece 5-1/2" from each long side, as shown. (Fig. 5-11) Butt the folded edges together in the middle of the bag piece and top-stitch the webbing

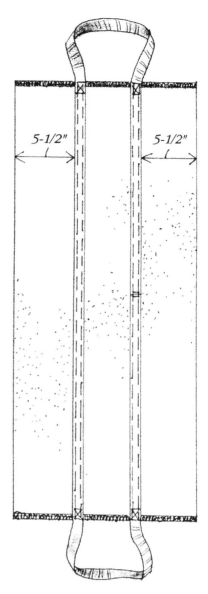

Fig. 5-11: Position the straps on the bag. Top-stitch the edges. Reinforce with square boxes and cross-stitching.

on both sides to secure. Reinforce the handles at the top edges of the bag by top-stitching square boxes, then cross-stitch diagonally. The handles will be about 14", allowing the bag to be carried comfortably without dragging on the ground. If you purchase the longer webbing yardage to make a shoulder bag, the straps will be about 27".

5. With right sides together, fold the bag piece in half, matching the short ends. Serge-seam both sides, matching the binding at the top edge. If you used a 3-thread stitch, reinforce the seams with straight-stitching.

6. From the inside of the bag, fold the corners to points with the serging in the middle and straight-stitch a line 3" from the point, forming a triangle. (Fig. 5-12) This boxes the bottom of the bag.

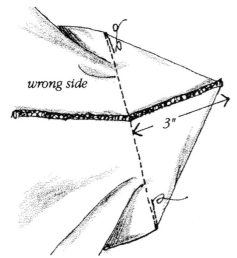

Fig. 5-12: *Straight-stitch inside corners at bottom of bag.*

7. At the top edge, press the seam allowances to one side and top-stitch parallel to the decorative stitching to reinforce and secure.

Lesson 14. Double-bound Edge

In Lesson 2 (page 44), you learned how to serge a double-bound seam. Fabric was folded over the seam allowances and then decoratively serge-finished. A similar technique is used to create a double-bound edge. Consider using it to trim garment edges or home decoration projects.

A double-bound edge can be serged either directly onto the fabric or onto a binding strip for later application. This edge takes a little more time (just like double-bound seams), but it makes an attractive and durable trim.

1. Cut out the project leaving an extra 1" allowance for all edges that will be double-bound.

2. Fold or press 3/4" to the wrong side on each edge.

3. Adjust for a wide 3- or 4-thread stitch and a very short, satin-stitch length. A 5mm stitch width will produce a binding almost 1/2" wide (twice the stitch width).

4. With decorative thread in the upper looper and the turned-back fold of the fabric next to the cutter, serge on the turned-back fold with the wrong side of the fabric on top. (Fig. 5-13)

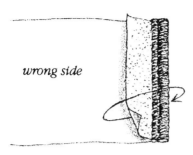

Fig. 5-13: Serge over the fold from the wrong side of the fabric to begin a double-bound edge. Fold the stitching to the right side and top-stitch.

5. Press the serged fold to the right side of the fabric and top-stitch to secure.

 Optional: Use fusible thread in the lower looper, then fuse to secure.

6. Fold the cut edge of the fabric toward the wrong side, forming a fold the exact width as your previous stitching.

7. Serge over the fold with the needleline on top of or right next to the needleline of the previous stitching. (Fig. 5-14)

Fig. 5-14: Fold the cut edge toward the wrong side. Serge over the fold, matching needlelines.

8. Trim away the excess allowance close to the stitching on the wrong side of the binding.

Project: Show-off Pillow

Double-bound edges accent a decorative inset piece on this fashionable pillow. We've embellished the contrasting inset fabric with diagonal rolled edges, but you may choose to show off any of your serger techniques. (Fig. 5-15)

Fig. 5-15: A pillow with double-bound edges and a decorative inset shows off serging skills.

Foot: Standard for binding and serge-seaming; rolled edge for inset
Plate: Standard for binding and serge-seaming; rolled edge for inset
Stitch: 3- or 4-thread for binding and serge-seaming; rolled edge for inset
Stitch length: Short (1-2mm)

Stitch width: Wide (4mm or 5mm) for binding and seaming; narrow (1.8mm or 2mm) for rolled edge on inset

Thread: Contrasting color
Needles: All-purpose or serger
Upper looper: Woolly nylon
Lower looper: All-purpose or serger thread; woolly nylon or monofilament nylon for rolled edge

Tension: Balanced for binding and serge-seaming; rolled edge for inset

Needle(s): Size 11/75

Fabric: 1/2 yard of velveteen or similar fabric; 1/4 yard of contrasting fabric for inset

Notions: 16" polyester pillow form

1. From the pillow fabric, cut one 16" by 16" square for the pillow back. Cut one 5" by 16" rectangle and one 8" by 16" rectangle for the pillow front. If you are using velveteen, make sure to cut all pieces with the nap going in the same direction.

2. Serge a double-bound edge along one long edge of both pillow front pieces. (Refer to the instructions on page 82.)

3. From the inset fabric, cut one 9" by 20" rectangle. Press-mark evenly spaced diagonal lines about 2-1/2" apart.

4. Adjust for a rolled-edge stitch and serge over all the press-marked lines.

5. Carefully press the decorated fabric. Cut the inset piece to a 6" by 16" rectangle.

6. Overlap each double-bound edge 1/2" over the long edges of the inset. Top-stitch to secure, completing the pillow front.

7. With the pillow front and the pillow back right sides together, serge-seam the edges with a wide, medium-length, balanced 3- or 4-thread stitch. Leave an 8" opening at the lower edge to insert the pillow form. Turn right side out. After inserting the pillow form, edge-stitch or hand-tack the opening closed.

Lesson 15.
Serged Piping

Traditionally, piping is made by tightly covering a cord with fabric, leaving a seam allowance for inserting the piping into a garment or project seam. We can easily replicate traditional piping by serging over filler cord onto a strip of 1-1/4"-wide bias tricot, such as *Seams Great*.

1. Thread the upper looper with decorative thread and adjust for a rolled edge with a short, satin-length stitch. Change to the rolled-edge plate but use either the standard or piping presser foot. (The piping foot can be used to make piping as well as insert it because it has the same hole placement as the standard presser foot.)

2. Serge over one or more strands of heavy thread or cording. Place the filler through one of the presser foot holes and out under the back of the foot. Refer back to Lesson 4 (page 54) for tips on serging over filler cord.

Special Tips: If your rolled edge is not completely wrapping to the underside, use monofilament or woolly nylon thread in the lower looper. You may need to increase the stitch width if you are serging over several strands of heavy thread or a thick cord. You might also need to increase the stitch length if you have heavy decorative thread in your upper looper.

3. Serge over the filler for several inches, then insert the bias tricot strip under the presser foot. Serge over the strip, trimming about 1/2" with the cutters. Do not stretch while serging. At the end, raise the presser foot, clear the stitch finger manually or by pressing the tension-release lever, and chain off over the filler.

The filler cord itself may also be used as an ornamental element. Serge

monofilament
nylon thread

1-1/4"
Seams
Great

decorative
filler cord

decorative filler piping

clear
elastic

satin
rolled
edge

elasticized
piping

Fig. 5-16: Serged piping options include featuring the filler cord itself and stretchable piping.

over decorative thread, ribbon, or braid using monofilament nylon in the upper looper and a longer stitch length. (Fig. 5-16)

Create a stretchable serged piping for stretch and knit garments by using clear elastic in place of the bias tricot. Stretch the elastic slightly while serge-piping along one edge.

Finished piping is traditionally inserted in a garment or project seam using a straight-stitch and a zipper foot. But the *Superlock* piping foot allows you to guide and insert the piping and serge-finish the seam allowance in one simple step.

Project: Serge-piped Book Cover

Cover your current paperback book with style. Serged piping accents the upper and lower edges. A matching satin rolled edge finishes the inner edges. (Fig. 5-17)

Fig. 5-17: Make an easy paperback book cover featuring contrasting piping. Give one as a thoughtful gift or show it off yourself.

Foot: Piping
Plate: Rolled edge for piping and trim; standard for serge-seaming
Stitch: 3-thread for rolled-edge piping and trim; 3- or 4-thread for serge-seaming
Stitch length: Short (1-2mm) for piping and trim; medium (2.5-3mm) for serge-seaming
Stitch width: Narrow for piping and trim; wide for serge-seaming
Thread: Contrasting color
  Needle(s): All-purpose or serger
  Upper looper: #8 pearl cotton for piping and trim; all-purpose or serger for serge-seaming
  Lower looper: Monofilament nylon for piping and trim; all-purpose or serger for serge-seaming
  Filler: 4 strands of #5 pearl cotton, the same color as the upper looper thread
Tension: Rolled edge for piping and trim; balanced for serge-seaming
Needle(s): Size 14/90
Fabric: 1/4 yard denim
Notions: 2 yards of 1-1/4" *Seams Great*; 10" of 3/8"-wide ribbon to match the piping (for a bookmark)

1. Cut a 16-1/2" by 8" rectangle from the denim.

2. With a satin-length, rolled-edge stitch and decorative thread in the upper looper, serge-finish both short ends of the rectangle, creating a trim.

3. Using the same stitch, serge over the four strands of #5 pearl cotton onto the *Seams Great* to make at least 24" of serged piping.

4. For the upper edge, cut an 11" section of piping. On one end, trim the *Seams Great* allowance to 1/4" for about 2". Place the piping on the 1/4" seamline on the right side of one long edge, as shown. (Fig. 5-18)

Fig. 5-18: Serge-seam the piping to the cover, starting and ending 3" from each end.

5. Matching cut edges, pin one end of the ribbon on the wrong side at the center of the edge.

6. Adjust for a 3- or 4-thread balanced stitch using all-purpose or serger thread. Serge-finish the edge for 3". Then serge onto the piping, positioning it in the groove of the foot and leaving a 1" tail, as shown. Serge-seam the piping to the cover until 3" from the end. Pull the piping tail to the left, behind the needle, and complete the edge by serge-finishing.

7. Repeat steps 4 and 6 for the lower edge. (Skip step 5.)

8. Fold 3" to the right side on each end. Matching the cut edges, serge-seam over the previous stitching (still using the piping foot), pulling the piping tails in the direction of the seam allowances at each corner. (Fig. 5-19)

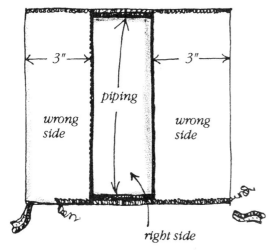

Fig. 5-19: *Fold back cover pockets and serge-seam over the previous stitching. Piping tails are pulled to the wrong side of the cover.*

9. Turn the cover to the right side and top-stitch next to the piping along the upper and lower edges.

 Optional: If you don't have a piping foot, use your standard presser foot. Serge-finish both long edges of the cover before applying the piping. Use a sewing machine zipper foot to straight-stitch the piping into position on both long edges. Then fold the 3" pockets and straight-stitch them along the piping stitching line. Trim the *Seams Great* close to the stitching before turning the cover right side out.

Lesson 16.
Mock Piping

Like serged piping, mock piping is made by covering filler cord with a satin rolled edge. It is not considered actual piping, however, because it is serged directly onto the fabric instead of being applied to a bias strip and inserted into a seam. We often see mock piping used as a decorative detail on lightweight robes, pajamas, and casual wear.

To create a simple mock-piped edge, serge along the seamline on the right side of the fabric using a satin rolled edge. Mock piping can be serged single-layer on more stable fabrics or double-layer (wrong sides together). (Fig. 5-20)

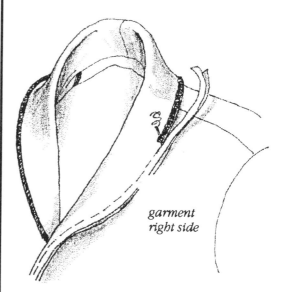

Fig. 5-20: *Create mock piping by serge-finishing the edges, wrong sides together, with a satin rolled edge.*

On lightweight material, the fabric edge will roll inside the stitching, creating a piped appearance without filler cord. On heavier fabrics, it may not be possible to roll the edge. In this case, loosen the upper looper and adjust for a narrow, satin-length, reversible-edge binding stitch (page 69). Inserting filler cord will add to the piped effect.

A variation of the mock-piped edge is used to create mock-piped bands and cuffs on lightweight fabrics.

1. Fold the band or cuff lengthwise with wrong sides together.

2. Place the band to the wrong side of the fabric, matching the cut edges.

3. Serge mock piping with the band on top. (Fig. 5-21)

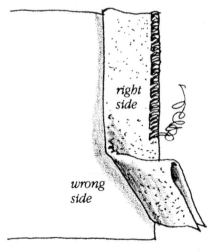

Fig. 5-21: *For mock piping, place the wrong side of the band against the wrong side of the fabric. Serge-seam with a satin rolled edge.*

4. Pull the seam flat and press the allowances away from the band or cuff.

Another mock-piping variation can be used to hem sleeves and lower edges.

1. Lightly press 1/4" to the wrong side. Then press the hem allowance to the wrong side. This technique looks best with a hem allowance of 1" or more. If the hem allowance on your pattern is narrower, add a wider allowance when cutting out the project.

2. Make another fold to the wrong side equal to the hem allowance, sandwiching the 1/4" edge toward the inside of the fold, as shown. (Fig. 5-22)

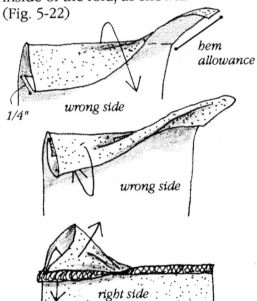

Fig. 5-22: *For a mock-piped hem, press 1/4" and then the hem allowance to the wrong side. Fold again and serge with a satin rolled edge. Pull the seam flat.*

3. From the right side, serge over the fold with the satin rolled edge, being careful not to cut the fabric.

4. Pull the seam flat and press the allowances away from the folded hem edge. The cut edge will be encased inside the hem.

Project: Easy Mock-piped Apron

The bib and lower edge of this simple apron are decoratively hemmed with mock piping. The ties sport mock-piped edges. (Fig. 5-23)

Fig. 5-23: Mock serged piping highlights hemlines and ties on this easy but serviceable apron.

Foot: Rolled edge for mock piping; standard for serge-finishing
Plate: Rolled edge for mock piping; standard for serge-finishing
Stitch: 3-thread
Stitch length: Short (1-2mm) for mock piping; medium (2.5-3mm) for serge-finishing
Stitch width: Narrow (1.8mm or 2mm) for mock piping; medium (2.8mm or 3.5mm) for serge-finishing
Thread: Contrasting color for mock piping; matching for serge-finishing
Needle: All-purpose or serger
Upper looper: Woolly nylon for mock piping; all-purpose or serger for serge-finishing
Lower looper: Woolly nylon or monofilament nylon for mock piping; all-purpose or serger for serge-finishing
Tension: Rolled edge for mock piping; balanced for serge-finishing
Needle: Size 11/75
Fabric: 1 yard 45" cotton/polyester woven

1. Cut one 14" by 17" rectangle and one 24" square for the apron. Cut two 30" by 3" and two 27" by 2" ties.

2. Adjust your serger for a balanced serge-finishing stitch.

3. Serge-finish the two long edges of the rectangle and three edges of the square.

4. Press each finished edge 1" to the wrong side and top-stitch 3/4" from the fold.

5. Fold each tie lengthwise with wrong sides together and serge-finish one short end.

6. Adjust your serger for mock piping. (See instructions on page 87.)

7. Finish the long and unfinished short edges of the ties with a mock-piped edge.

8. Hem the upper and lower edge of the bib and the lower edge of the apron using the mock-piped hem technique on page 88. The hem allowance is 2".

9. Lap the narrower ties 1" under the corners of the upper bib edge. Top-stitch in a square to secure. Lap and top-stitch the wider ties 1" under each corner of the upper edge of the apron. (Fig. 5-24)

top-stitching

lap and top-stitch
all four edges

Fig. 5-24: Top-stitch the ties to the apron. Lap the bib over the apron and top-stitch through all layers.

10. Center and lap the bib over the upper edge of the apron, aligning the mock piping with the edge. Top-stitch all four edges.

Lesson 17.
Serged Trim

It is often difficult to find just the right decorative trim for your fashion or project. Now you have a wide range of options for designing and serging your own. The base fabric width, content, and color can be varied. And you can use a large assortment of thread types and colors. Any decorative edging stitch is a possibility. Always test first.

1. Select a bias strip of woven fabric or a cross-grain strip of knit that matches or contrasts with the fabric you are binding. Cut the length you'll need plus 1". The width of the bias strip should measure your desired finished trim width plus 1/2". For a 3/4"-wide trim, you'll need a strip 1-1/4" wide.

2. On one long edge, press 1/4" to the wrong side.

3. Adjust your serger for a balanced 3-thread stitch or any other decorative stitch you would like on your trim.

4. With decorative thread in the upper looper and the fold next to the cutter, serge carefully along the fold without cutting the fabric. Use a blindhem foot for easiest guiding.

 Special Tip: For easiest finishing, use fusible thread in the lower looper and a medium to wide, balanced stitch.

5. Place the decorative side of the strip against the wrong side of the project fabric, aligning the cut edges.

6. Using all-purpose serger thread serge the edge with a 1/4" seam. If your stitch is not that wide, serge-seam and straight-stitch at the 1/4" seamline. (Fig. 5-25)

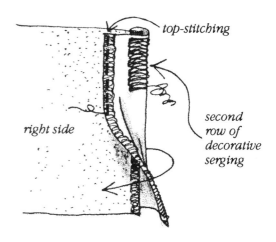

Fig. 5-26: Add more color and texture to serged trim with a wider binding. Then decoratively serge again after folding and securing the binding on the right side.

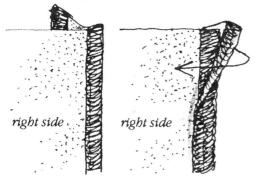

Fig. 5-25: Decoratively serge the binding strip, using fusible thread in the lower looper. Serge-seam the strip to the fabric, then wrap decorative serging to the right side and fuse.

7. Wrap the trim to the right side, encasing the seam.

8. Carefully press the trim in place and top-stitch to secure. If you've used fusible thread, carefully fuse the trim in place. Then top-stitching is optional but adds durability.

9. To add more texture or color to your trim, you may choose to use a wider binding and decoratively serge over the folded edge (without cutting it). Use a different stitch or stitch width for variety. (Fig. 5-26)

Project: Serged-Trim Table Runner

Add elegance to a special dinner party with an easily constructed table runner. It is neatly serge-finished with narrow single-edged trim. A tassel ornaments each end. (Fig. 5-27)

Fig. 5-27: Metallic serged trim highlights an easy, yet elegant, table runner.

Foot: Standard

Plate: Standard

Stitch: 3-thread for decorative; 3- or 4-thread for serge-seaming

Stitch length: Short (1-2mm) for decorative; medium (2.5-3mm) for serge-seaming

Stitch width: Wide (4mm or 5mm)

Thread: Contrasting color

    Needle(s): All-purpose or serger

    Upper looper: Metallic yarn for decorative; all-purpose or serger for serge-seaming

    Lower looper: All-purpose, serger, or fusible for decorative; all-purpose or serger for serge-seaming

Tension: Balanced

Needle(s): Size 14/75

Fabric: 2 yards tapestry or heavy brocade for 70" length (or 2-1/2 yards for a 90" length); one yard of matching lightweight satin for binding

1. Cut a 20" by 70" or 90" rectangle (depending on the measurements of your table) from the runner fabric.

2. Fold the fabric in half lengthwise. At each end, fold the corner back and press-mark a bias line. (Fig. 5-28) Cut on this line to form the end points.

Fig. 5-28: *Fold the fabric lengthwise, then align the short edges back against the folds and press-mark. Cut on the press marks to form points.*

3. Cut and splice 1-1/4"-wide bias strips of the matching lightweight satin to make a trim the length of the runner perimeter plus 1". On one long edge, carefully press 1/4" to the wrong side.

4. Adjust your serger for a short, wide, balanced stitch and decoratively serge the folded edge.

5. Along one side of the table runner (from point to point), serge the cut edge of the right side of the trim to the wrong side of the fabric. If your serger does not have a 1/4" seaming width, straight-stitch on the 1/4" seamline. Wrap the serged-trim binding to the right side and top-stitch. (Fig. 5-29)

Fig. 5-29: *Apply serged-trim binding to one side of the runner. Serge-seam the opposite edge. Fold back the corners to miter before top-stitching.*

Optional: Use fusible thread in the lower looper of the decorative stitching and fuse instead of top-stitching.

6. Repeat step 5 for the opposite edge of the runner. Before wrapping the binding to the right side, fold back the corners on each end to form miters. Then top-stitch to secure.

7. Cover the end points and reinforce them with tassels by following the instructions in Lesson 35 (page 153).

Lesson 18. Serge-piped Binding

A popular variation of the serged trim in Lesson 15 is constructed with a narrow rolled edge and a satin-stitch length. This binding gives the appearance of piping without the extra steps of inserting a piping strip. Serge-piped binding makes a pretty, delicate finish on lightweight or silky fabric—great for neckline and sleeve edges.

1. Cut a bias strip of woven fabric or a cross-grain strip of knit for the binding. Cut the length you'll need plus 1". The width of the bias strip should measure your desired finished trim width plus 3/4". For a 1/2" finished binding, cut the binding strips 1-1/4" wide.

2. On one long edge, press 1/4" to the wrong side. (Fig. 5-30)

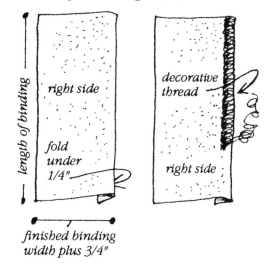

Fig. 5-30: Make serge-piped binding by pressing 1/4" to the wrong side and serging a rolled edge on the fold.

3. Serge-finish the fold with a narrow rolled edge, adjusted to a short, satin-stitch length. Use decorative thread in the upper looper and matching all-purpose or serger thread in the needle and lower looper. Shiny rayon thread is a good choice for silky fabric because it complements the fabric texture.

4. Place the right side of the binding to the wrong side of the project fabric with cut edges matching.

5. Serge a 1/4" seam. If your widest serged stitch is narrower than 1/4", serge-seam and then straight-stitch at the 1/4" seamline. (Fig. 5-31)

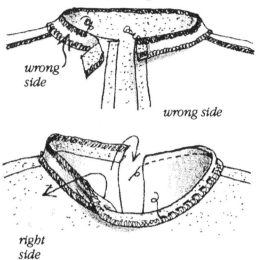

Fig. 5-31: Serge the binding to the wrong side of the edge. Wrap it to the right side and straight-stitch along the rolled-edge needleline.

6. Fold the binding to the right side and straight-stitch on top of the rolled-edge needleline. Use a zipper foot to help position your stitches accurately.

Project: Padded Picture Frame

Serge-piped binding finishes the inside oval edge of this pretty 5" by 7" picture frame. Enlarge the measurements to fit a larger photo. (The binding is more difficult to apply for a frame smaller than 5" by 7".) (Fig. 5-32)

Fig. 5-32: A padded picture frame is trimmed with serge-piped binding.

Foot: Rolled edge for decorative; standard for serge-finishing
Plate: Rolled edge for decorative; standard for serge-finishing
Stitch: 3-thread rolled edge for decorative; 3-thread balanced for serge-finishing
Stitch length: Satin for decorative; short (1-2mm) for serge-finishing
Stitch width: Narrow (1.8mm or 2mm)
Thread: Contrasting color
  Needle(s): All-purpose or serger
  Upper looper: Rayon for decorative; all-purpose or serger for serge-finishing
  Lower looper: Woolly nylon for decorative; all-purpose or serger for serge-finishing

Tension: Rolled edge for decorative; balanced for serge-finishing
Needle(s): Size 11/75
Fabric: 1/3 yard 45"-wide woven
Notions: 1/4 yard fusible transfer web; 8" by 10" polyester bonded batting; one file folder; 6" by 8" of 1/8"-thick cardboard; 5-3/4" by 7-3/4" clear acetate sheet (from a school or office-supply store); hot glue gun and glue

1. From the fabric, cut two 8" by 10" rectangles, one 6" by 8" rectangle, and one bias strip 1-1/4" by 18". From the transfer web, cut one 8" by 10" rectangle and one 5-1/2" by 7-1/2" rectangle.

2. To make the frame, cut a 6" by 8" rectangle from the file folder. Cut a 4" by 6" oval opening in the center of the rectangle, as shown. (Fig. 5-33)

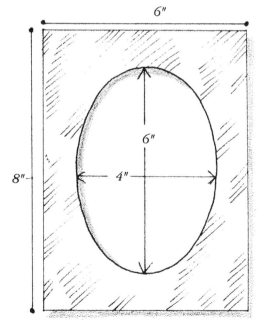

Fig. 5-33: From the file folder, cut a rectangle with an oval in the center.

3. Center and fuse together one 8" by 10" fabric piece, the 8" by 10" transfer web, the batting, the 5-1/2" by 7-1/2" transfer web, and the cardboard frame, as shown. (Fig. 5-34)

Fig. 5-34: Fuse the layers to the front of the frame. Cut out along the oval edge after fusing.

4. Cut out the batting and fabric inside the oval right at the opening edge. Fold the fused layers to the back of the frame on all four outer edges and glue in place.

5. For the binding, press 1/4" to the wrong side along one long edge of the bias strip. With decorative thread in the upper looper, serge-finish over the fold with a rolled-edge stitch. Serge about 6" of extra chain, leaving thread tails at the ends. The chain will be used for hanging the finished picture frame.

6. On one short end, fold the bias strip 3/8" to the wrong side. On the file-folder side, beginning at the lower right edge of the oval, place the right side of the folded end of the binding against the frame, matching the cut edges. Straight-stitch the binding to the frame around the oval opening using a 1/4" seam allowance. (You will be stitching through the file folder, as well as through the fabric and batting.) Lap the end of the strip over the beginning fold as you complete the seam. (Fig. 5-35)

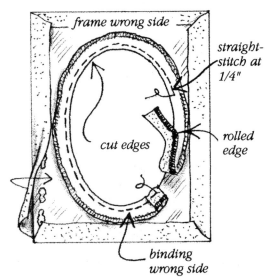

Fig. 5-35: *Sew the right side of the binding to the wrong side of the frame.*

7. Fold the binding evenly to the right side. Straight-stitch on the rolled-edge needleline to secure.

8. Make the frame back by folding the other 8" by 10" fabric piece over the heavier cardboard. Glue the edges to secure.

9. With a narrow, balanced 3-thread stitch, serge-finish the 6" by 8" fabric piece, trimming approximately 1/8" from all sides. Glue the serge-finished piece over the fabric edges on the cardboard back.

10. Use the rolled-edge chain made in step 5 for hanging. Hand-tack each end to the serge-finishing stitches on both sides of the frame back, about 2-1/2" down from the top edge.

11. Apply hot glue around two sides and the bottom of both frame pieces—on the front side of the covered cardboard and the back side of the frame front. Keep the glue within 1/4" of the edge. Sandwich the clear acetate between the two glued pieces and apply pressure until dry. (Fig. 5-36)

Fig. 5-36: *Glue the sides and bottom of the frame pieces, sandwiching the acetate sheet between.*

12. The flower made in Lesson 24 (page 118) will cover the binding overlap and complete the frame.

Lesson 19.
Double Rolled-edge Braid and Binding

The double rolled edge featured in Lesson 5 (page 60) can be adapted to make both a narrow braid and a decorative binding. Using contrasting thread colors for the two rolled edges accents the delicate technique. Because maximum thread coverage and a perfectly rolled edge are important, we often choose woolly nylon for both the upper and lower loopers.

Double rolled-edge braid

To make double rolled-edge braid for trimming your garments, home decorations, or craft projects, serge over a 1/2" strip of base fabric. Choose any lightweight fabric that matches or blends with the upper looper thread color.

1. Adjust your serger for a satin rolled edge.

2. Serge one long edge of the fabric strip, leaving a thread chain several inches long.

3. Rethread the upper looper with a contrasting thread color. Serge the other side of the strip with the needle on or right next to the needleline of the original serging. (Fig. 5-37) Hold the thread chain taut to start the serging without jamming. Aligning

Fig. 5-37: *Make a double rolled-edge braid trim by serging two rows of rolled edging on a fabric strip, aligning the needlelines.*

the needlelines and perfecting this technique may take a little practice.

 Special Tip: Use the *Superlock* piping foot for the easiest double rolled edge. (See Lesson 5, page 60.)

4. Top-stitch the braid to your project fabric, stitching directly on the center needleline.

Double rolled-edge binding

A matching decorative binding is made by serge-finishing the folded edge of a bias-woven or a cross-grain knit binding strip using a double rolled-edge technique. Choose a lightweight fabric that matches or blends with the thread colors and the fabric to be bound.

1. Cut and splice the binding strip twice your finished binding width plus 1-1/2" by the length you'll need for your project. Fold the strip in half lengthwise with wrong sides together.

2. Serge the fold with a satin rolled edge. From the wrong side, press the binding open.

3. Rethread the upper looper with a contrasting thread color. Then refold the binding strip and serge-finish the edge with the needlelines on top of, or right next to, each other. (Fig. 5-38)

align needlelines

right side

Fig. 5-38: *For double rolled-edge binding, serge-finish a fold. Then refold and serge an adjoining rolled edge.*

 Optional: Use the piping foot for added accuracy.

4. Place the right side of the binding to the wrong side of the fabric, matching the cut edges. Serge-seam with your widest stitch or straight-stitch a 1/4" seam. If you are applying the binding to an outside curve, ease the binding around the curve.

5. Press the binding to the right side and top-stitch between the rolled-edge rows to secure. (Fig. 5-39)

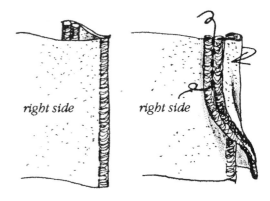

right side   *right side*

Fig. 5-39: *Serge-seam double rolled-edge binding to the fabric edge. Wrap it to the right side and top-stitch on the center needleline.*

Project: Tooth Fairy Pillow

Double rolled-edge binding finishes the pocket and edges of this special little pillow. The tooth fairy will know just where to find the lost tooth and leave a reward. (Fig. 5-40)

Fig. 5-40: *This special tooth fairy pillow is trimmed with double rolled-edge binding.*

Foot: Piping or standard
Plate: Rolled edge for decorative; standard for serge-seaming
Stitch: 3-thread for decorative; 3- or 4-thread for serge-seaming
Stitch length: Short (1mm) for decorative; medium (2.5-3mm) for serge-seaming
Stitch width: Narrow (1.8mm or 2mm) for decorative; medium for serge-seaming
Thread: Contrasting colors
    Needle(s): All-purpose or serger
    Upper looper: Two contrasting colors of woolly nylon for decorative; all-purpose or serger for serge-seaming
    Lower looper: Woolly nylon for decorative; all-purpose or serger for serge-seaming
Tension: Rolled edge for decorative; balanced for serge-seaming
Needle(s): Size 11/75
Fabric: 1/6 yard 45"-wide woven; 2-1/2" by 27" matching or contrasting bias strip
Notions: Approximately one handful of polyester fiberfill; 12" of 1/8"-wide ribbon for bow

1. Cut two 4-1/2" by 5-1/2" rectangles for the pillow and one 4-1/2" by 3-1/2" rectangle for the pocket. Place the pocket over the two pillow pieces and match the cut edges at one end. Using a cup, round all four corners. (Fig. 5-41)

Fig. 5-41: *Place the smaller rectangle over the two larger rectangles and round the corners.*

2. Make double rolled-edge binding on the bias strip following the instructions on page 97. Trim the strip width to 1".

3. Bind the upper (straight) edge of the pocket by applying the right side of the binding to the wrong side of the pocket. Wrap the binding to the right side and top-stitch on the rolled-edge needleline.

4. Place the pillow pieces wrong sides together with the pocket on the top, matching the cut edges. Serge-seam around the pillow with a medium- to wide-width (3.5mm to 5mm) balanced stitch. Leave an opening at the top for inserting the fiberfill. Stuff the pillow and serge-seam the opening closed.

5. On one short end, fold the binding strip 1/2" to the wrong side. Beginning in the middle of the top edge, place the right side of the folded end of the binding against the back side of the pillow, matching the cut edges. Serge with a 1/4" seam allowance, lapping the end of the strip over the beginning fold as you complete the seam. If your serger does not have a stitch that wide, straight-stitch on the 1/4" seamline after serging.

6. Fold the binding to the right side and top-stitch on the rolled-edge needleline to secure.

7. Add a bow at the top of the pillow to cover the binding joint.

Lesson 20. Elasticized Trims and Binding

The serger makes sewing stretch and knit fabrics a breeze. Now you can also serge elasticized trims and binding to add decorative detail and to individualize your garments.

Elasticized trims

A classic example of new products leading to new techniques, serging elasticized trim was never an option before the introduction of clear elastic. Now we can make a variety of stretch trims to coordinate with any stretch or knit fabric. Using different stitch widths, tension adjustments, and thread types adds to the possibilities.

Because clear elastic is so lightweight, it is important to serge through it to keep it from rolling. Neatly trim any excess elastic after serging the trim. The *Superlock* elastic foot works well for the 1/4" and 3/8" widths. Loosen the foot's screw so no tension is placed on the elastic.

Single-stretch Trim

1. Begin with a single row of serging on a piece of clear elastic. Test various widths.

2. Adjust the stitch width to the width of braid desired. The elastic width must be wider than the stitch width.

3. Serge, using a short (not satin) 2mm stitch length. For better coverage, use woolly nylon in both loopers.

4. Adjust the tension for a balanced 3-thread stitch, making it loose enough to allow the elastic to lie flat. After serging several inches, test the braid by stretching. If the stitches break, loosen the needle thread tension or stretch the elastic slightly as you serge.

5. If you're not using an elastic foot, hold the elastic taut in front of and behind the presser foot while serging. It is not necessary to stretch because the serged stitch allows for stretch.

6. Trim the elastic close to the serging, being careful not to cut the stitches. (Fig. 5-42) If part of the elastic still remains, it won't show when the trim is top-stitched to the garment.

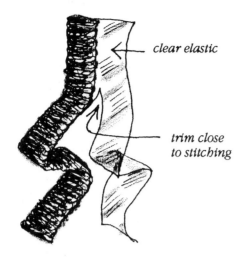

Fig. 5-42: Decoratively serge clear elastic, then trim it close to the stitching to make single-stretch trim.

Fig. 5-43: Double-stretch trim features a second row of serging with needlelines aligned.

7. Top-stitch the trim to the garment, using a long stitch and sewing close to each edge of the trim. Stretch the elastic as you sew.

Double-stretch Trim

Select an elastic that is wider than the trim you will be making.

1. Serge one side of the elastic following the above guidelines, except do not trim the elastic.

2. On the opposite (unserged) side, serge another row with the needle just inside or next to the needleline of the previous stitching. (Fig. 5-43) For variation, use a different thread color in the upper looper when serging the second side.

3. Top-stitch the trim to the garment using a long stitch and sewing close to each edge of the trim. Stretch the elastic as you sew.

Stretch-trim Variations

Adjust your serger for a narrow (1.8mm or 2mm), balanced stitch. Tighten the lower looper tension slightly. Serge the elastic, following the directions for the double-stretch trim above.

Try serging a balanced stitch on one side and a rolled-edge stitch on the other side. Or serge a rolled edge on both sides, overlapping the needlelines. (Fig. 5-44) For more elasticity

Fig. 5-44: Stretch-trim variations include double trim with one or two rolled edges.

when serging a rolled edge on clear elastic, stretch the elastic. It will return to its original length after serging.

Braided Trim

Braid the elastic trim for swimsuit or camisole straps:

1. Serge a strand of single-stretch trim six times the length of the strap plus 6".

2. Cut the trim into six equal lengths. Braid it into two straps and secure the ends with straight-stitching. (Fig. 5-45)

3. Attach the straps to your garment according to the pattern guidesheet.

Elasticized binding

This technique adds stretch and stability to an edge and creates a neat, decorative binding at the same time. You have the option of leaving one serged-finished edge exposed on the under side of the binding or wrapping and twin-needle top-stitching to leave no serged edges exposed.

Elasticized binding works especially well on stretch fabrics because the serged stitch used to apply the elastic is a stretch stitch. Use it to finish the edges of swim or exercisewear. You can even extend the binding past the garment edge to form straps. Any width elastic may be used, but 3/8" is the most versatile. Select any type except clear elastic. (It will roll inside the binding.)

To bind the edge of stretch fabric:

1. Cut the elastic to the desired length. Cut a stretch binding strip the same length. Its width should be three times the width of the elastic plus 1/4". For a heavy or thick fabric, cut the strip an additional 1/4" wider.

Fig. 5-45: Braided stretch trim is used for swimsuit and camisole straps.

2. Serge-finish one long edge of the strip using a medium width and length 3-thread stitch, trimming only slightly to neaten.

3. Place the right sides of the binding and fabric together, matching the cut edges. Straight-stitch with a seam allowance the width of the elastic (usually 3/8"). Stretch the layers as you sew. (Fig. 5-46)

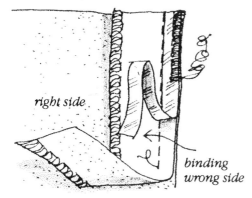

Fig. 5-46: For elasticized binding, straight-stitch the binding to the garment, stretching both layers. Serge elastic to the seam allowance on top of the binding.

4. Adjust the serger for a long, balanced 3-thread stitch. Place the elastic on top of the binding, next to the edge. Serge it to the seam allowance through all layers.

5. Fold the binding to the wrong side, encasing the serged seam allowance. From the right side, top-stitch on the binding with a narrow zigzag or a twin needle to secure, stretching slightly as you sew. (Fig. 5-47) Or stitch-in-the-ditch from the right side, stretching firmly.

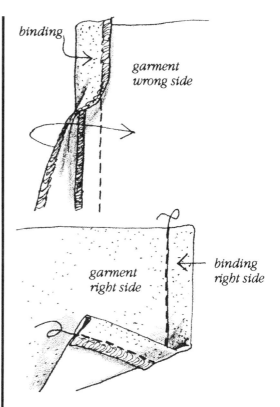

Fig. 5-47: Fold the binding to the wrong side and top-stitch or stitch-in-the-ditch.

 Optional: To make a binding with no exposed serging, the width of the binding strip should be four times the width of the elastic plus 1/4". Don't serge-finish one long edge. After applying (steps 3 and 4), fold the unsewn edge of the binding 3/8" (the width of the seam allowance) to the wrong side, matching the cut edge to the serged edge.

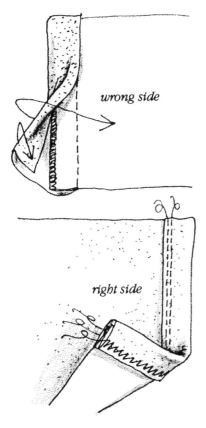

wrong side

right side

Fig. 5-48: *For elasticized binding with no exposed serging, fold the unsewn edge to the wrong side and wrap it to encase the elastic. Top-stitch or stitch-in-the-ditch to secure.*

Fold 3/8" again, encasing the serged elastic. From the right side, top-stitch the binding with a narrow zigzag or a twin needle. (Fig. 5-48)

The application of elasticized binding varies slightly from stretch fabrics to wovens. When elasticized binding is applied to the edge of woven fabric, the fabric is gathered in with the elastic, so the binding must be cut larger than the opening.

1. Cut the elastic smaller than the opening, to the desired length.

2. If you are applying the binding to a curved area, cut the trim strip on the bias to allow it to lie smoothly.

3. Straight-stitch the binding to the fabric without stretching.

4. When applying the elastic, stretch the elastic to fit the length of the binding as you serge.

5. Finish as instructed for the stretch binding.

Project:
Ruffled Jar Cover

Serged elastic trim tucks this decorative cover around any jar lid. A ribbon bow adds a pretty finishing touch. (Fig. 5-49)

Fig. 5-49: *This ruffled jar cover has serged clear-elastic trim.*

Foot: Elastic or standard for elastic trim; rolled edge for serge-finishing

Plate: Standard for elastic trim; rolled edge for serge-finishing

Stitch: 3-thread

Stitch length: Short (1-2mm)

Stitch width: Narrow (1.8mm or 2mm)

Thread: Contrasting color
   Needle: All-purpose or serger
   Upper looper: Woolly nylon
   Lower looper: All-purpose or serger

Tension: Balanced for braid trim; rolled edge for serge-finishing

Needle: Size 11/75

Fabric: 1/4 yard gingham (or 8" by 8" square)

Notions: 12" of 1/4"- or 3/8"-wide clear elastic; 12" of 1/8"-wide ribbon; air-erasable marker

1. Cut an 8" circle from the gingham, using a lid or plate as a guide. With a smaller lid, mark a 5-1/2" circle inside the larger one using an air-erasable marker.

2. Serge-finish the edge of the larger circle with a rolled edge.

3. Serge along one edge of the elastic with a narrow satin stitch. If available, use an elastic foot with the tension screw loosened. Trim the unsewn elastic close to the serging.

4. Pin-mark the inner circle in halves and the elastic trim at 3-1/2" and 7". Place the elastic on the circle and straight-stitch through it with a long stitch, stretching to fit the markings. (Fig. 5-50) Finish by lapping the end over the beginning of the trim.

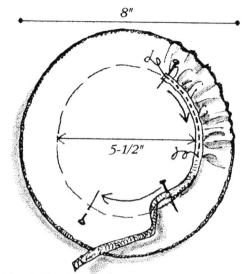

Fig. 5-50: Stretch the clear elastic trim while top-stitching.

5. Tie the ribbon into a bow and hand-tack it over the joined ends of the elastic.

Lesson 21. Puffed Serged Braid

A thread chain serged from heavy decorative thread can be used as ornamental braid. Serging over several strands of filler (as described in previous lessons) makes a heavier braid. For an even chunkier, puffed braid, serge over rolled fabric or thick yarn.

A strip of 1"-wide tricot, T-shirt knit, or jersey (cut on the crosswise grain) can be used for the puff-braid filler. Or use 5/8"-wide *Seams Great* for a more delicate braid. When pulled, the fabric strip rolls into a narrow tube and serger stitches can be formed around it. The resulting puffed braid is ideal for edging, couching, and craft projects.

Use decorative thread in the upper and lower looper with matching all-purpose or serger thread in the needle. Use heavier decorative thread when serging over thicker fabric such as jersey; use finer thread for serging over lightweight filler.

For a heavier braid, remove the presser foot. Use a *Superlock* pearl sewing foot if the braid is smaller and will fit through the guides.

1. Pull the fabric strip slightly so it rolls into a tube.

2. Place the tube between the needle and the cutter. Lower the presser-foot lever. If using the pearl foot, allow approximately an inch of the tube to extend in back of the foot.

3. Hold the end of the tube taut behind the pearl foot to prevent jamming as you begin to serge. If you are not using a foot, carefully guide the taut tube between the needle and cutter as you serge.

4. Continue to hold the serged braid taut (but ***don't*** pull), guiding it smoothly out behind the foot or needle. The stitches should form around, and not through, the tube. (Fig. 5-51)

Fig. 5-51: Make puffed serged braid by serging around a fabric tube or chunky yarn.

Puffed serged braid may be hand-tacked to your fabric to form a letter or design. Twist or braid strands together for a more pronounced trim. (Fig. 5-52)

Fig. 5-52: Puffed serged braid can be tacked or fused to fabric to form letters or designs. Twist or braid multiple strands for a pronounced effect.

S **Special Tip:** Use fusible thread in the lower looper to create fusible puffed braid. In most instances, the fusible thread will permanently bond the braid in place. For more durability, hand-tack the braid to the fabric, catching only the backside of the braid.

Project: Frog Closures

Heavy rayon thread is serged over a tube of wool jersey, then easily formed into traditional frog closures. Use two on the fringed scarf in Lesson 26 (page 124) or embellish your latest fashion garment. (Fig. 5-53)

Fig. 5-53: Make your own decorative frog closures with puffed serged braid.

Foot: None
Plate: Standard
Stitch: 3-thread
Stitch length: Medium (2.5-3mm)
Stitch width: Medium to wide (3.5-5mm)
Thread: Matching color
    Needle: All-purpose or serger
    Upper looper: Heavy rayon, like *Decor 6* or pearl rayon
    Lower looper: Woolly nylon
Tension: Balanced, with lower looper slightly tightened
Needle: Size 11/75
Fabric: Two 1" strips of 60"-wide wool or acrylic jersey, cut on the crosswise grain

1. Create puffed braid from the 60" jersey strips, following the instructions on page 106.

2. Cut two 10-1/2" strips and two 22" strips of the braid. Apply seam sealant to each end and allow it to dry.

3. From the short strips, form decorative loops, as shown. (Fig. 5-54) Hand-tack the braid together from the wrong side.

Fig. 5-54: Form the looped side of the closure and hand-tack the ends.

4. Using the longer strips, make a button with decorative loops matching those above. (Fig. 5-55) Hand-tack the braid together from the wrong side.

Fig. 5-55: Make a ball button, then form the tail into three decorative loops.

Lesson 22.
Serged Picot Braid

Create a delicate but stable picot braid by serging on water-soluble stabilizer. Using a heavy decorative thread in the upper looper and monofilament nylon thread in the lower looper creates the appearance of a looped single strand. After zig-zagging along the needleline and washing away the stabilizer, the braid may be glued to a craft project or accessory or top-stitched to a feminine blouse or dress.

1. Thread your serger with pearl cotton or crochet thread in the upper looper, monofilament nylon in the lower looper, and all-purpose or serger thread in the needle. Adjust for the longest, widest, balanced 3-thread stitch. For maximum width, try removing the upper looper thread from the tension controls. (For lay-in tension discs, place a strip of transparent tape over the slot.)

2. Serge-finish a strip of water-soluble stabilizer. To secure the serging, zigzag over the needleline with a narrow stitch and matching thread. (Fig. 5-56)

3. Trim the stabilizer about 1/8" from the serging.

4. Soak the braid in cold or luke-warm water, then lay it flat on a paper towel to dry. Or blot the braid with a paper towel to remove most of the moisture and dry it in a microwave oven on a medium power setting for approximately two minutes. (For safety, set the timer for one-minute intervals or less and check after each period.) Make sure the braid is as flat as possible while drying. When dry, press the braid flat using a press cloth.

water-soluble stabilizer

serge-finish   zigzag   trim, soak, dry, and press

Fig. 5-56: *To make picot braid, serge-finish water-soluble stabilizer. Zigzag over the needleline, trim the excess stabilizer, and soak the braid before drying and pressing.*

Project: Picot-trimmed Hat

Picot braid flowers transform a plain summer hat into a fashion statement. (Fig. 5-57)

Fig. 5-57: Picot braid flowers highlight a summer hat.

Foot: Standard
Plate: Standard
Stitch: 3-thread
Stitch length: Longest (5mm)
Stitch width: Wide (4mm or 5mm)
Thread: Contrasting color to hat
   Needle: All-purpose or serger
   Upper looper: Pearl cotton or
     crochet thread
   Lower looper: Monofilament
     nylon
Tension: Balanced
Needle: Size 11/75
Notions: One hat with large brim;
   6" by 27" piece of water-soluble
   stabilizer; clear-drying fabric glue

 Note: Each flower will use approximately 2/3 yard of braid. Serge four yards of braid for four flowers and select the best lengths for your project.

1. Thread and adjust your serger for picot braid following the instructions on page 108. Serge-finish one long edge of the stabilizer.

2. Zigzag over the needleline with a narrow stitch and matching thread.

3. Trim the stabilizer about 1/8" from the serging.

4. Soak the braid to remove the stabilizer. Then dry and press the braid.

5. Repeat steps 1 through 4 until you have enough yardage for your project.

6. Use a water-soluble marker to draw flower placement outlines on the hat.

7. Glue the picot braid onto the outlines, starting and ending in the center of each flower.

6. Special Decorative Serging Techniques

In past lessons you've mastered seams, edges, bindings, and trims. Now it's time to explore some of the special decorative techniques that make serger sewing so much fun. You can embellish fabric with flatlocking, trims, beading, and couching. You can gather, shirr, and fringe. You can even make a delicate, tatting-like lace with serger stitches.

Although decoratively serging seams and edges can ornament your latest fashion garments in high style, many more options are available. By serging along folds, you can add embellishment anywhere on your fabric. Practically any decorative technique you see in ready-to-wear can be duplicated.

The lessons in this chapter will lead you through some of our favorite serger applications. You'll be delighted with the number of additional ornamental serging possibilities they open up for you.

Lesson 23. Gathering and Shirring

We use several different methods of serge-gathering to create ruffles, attach full skirts to waistbands or bodices, and to ornament other serger projects. Although it is generally fast and easy, serge-gathering works best on projects that do not require the wider seam allowances used for couture tailoring or delicate fabrics.

The width of the serge-gathered seam allowance is limited by the width of the serged stitch. The weight or thickness of your fabric and the project itself help determine what method to use. With serge-gathering, a single layer of fabric will gather more than multiple layers.

Tension gathering

For easy gathering of lightweight fabric, tighten the needle tension almost all the way. Use a long stitch, your widest width, and a balanced 3-thread stitch. If you are using two needles, tighten both needle tensions. Vary the amount of gathers by changing the stitch length. A longer stitch length will gather the fabric more.

For speedier tension gathering, instead of tightening the tension controls, press the needle thread(s) against the face of your serger above the needle bar, as shown. (Fig. 6-1) This instant finger tensioning returns to normal just by releasing the threads.

Fig. 6-1: *To quickly gather lightweight fabric, apply tension to the needle thread.*

Differential-feed gathering

If your serger has differential feed, you can use it to easily gather light-weight fabrics. Use a wide, medium length, and balanced stitch. Adjust the differential feed to 2.0 for serge-gathering. To vary the amount of gathers, change the differential-feed setting or the length of the stitch. (The longest stitch you can use with the differential feed is 4mm.)

To softly gather only one layer or to ease when you are serging two layers, lengthen your stitch to 4mm. With the differential feed on 2.0, hold the top layer taut. On light- to medium-weight fabrics, the under layer will gather as you serge it to the top layer. Softer fabrics will gather more than stiff fabrics. Shorten your stitch length to reduce the amount of gathering.

Filler-cord gathering

To serge-gather medium- to heavy-weight fabrics, serge over a strand of filler thread such as buttonhole twist, crochet thread, or pearl cotton. (Fig. 6-2) Use a wide, medium to short

Fig. 6-2: *For medium- to heavy-weight fabric, serge over filler cord and pull to gather.*

(2.5mm), and balanced 3-thread stitch. Place the filler through the rear hole and under the back of the presser foot, guiding it with the techniques from Lesson 4 (page 54). Serge over the filler, being careful not to cut it. Secure one end of the filler and pull the other end to gather the edge.

If your serger has a 4-thread stitch, use both needles as you serge. Place the filler through the front presser-foot hole to guide it between the needles. (Fig. 6-3) The needle threads hold the filler in position for more controlled gathering.

Fig. 6-3: For more controlled gathering, place the filler thread between the two needles of a 4-thread stitch.

Thread-chain gathering

This technique uses thread chain as a gathering filler cord. Serge off a thread chain that is slightly longer than the edge to be gathered. Raise the presser foot and bring the chain under the back of the foot and then thread it up through the rear hole in the foot. Insert the fabric under the foot and serge over the chain as if you were using filler thread. Then draw the chain up to gather. Or hold the chain taut to gather as your serge.

Serge-shirring

Parallel rows of serge-shirring can create a stretchy waistband or cuffs on your latest fashion garments. We prefer shirring the fabric first, before cutting it out. In addition to gathering in fabric lengthwise, the serge-shirred stitching takes up extra fabric width— about twice the width of the serged stitch for each row of shirring.

For easiest serge-shirring, begin with a long strip of elastic thread, cord, or narrow clear elastic. (For more durability when shirring with elastic thread, serge over two or more strands.) Mark the desired length of your finished shirring on the elastic using a marking pen, leaving some extra at the beginning end. After serge-shirring over the elastic and fabric (see instructions next page), secure the unmarked end of elastic by pinning or sewing it and gather from the opposite end. (Fig. 6-4) Because

Fig. 6-4: Shirr accurately by marking the desired length on the elastic. Serge over the elastic, secure one end, and gather to the mark.

you've serged over the elastic, not into it, it will pull easily. When the mark is exposed, secure and trim that end of the elastic and adjust the shirring evenly.

To serge-shirr using *elastic thread or cord*, adjust your serger for a short (2.5mm), medium-width, and balanced 3-thread stitch. Place the thread through the rear hole and under the back of the presser foot as for the filler-cord gathering, page 111.

To begin, serge several stitches over the elastic until you reach the beginning mark you made. Fold the fabric right sides together and place it under the presser foot, using the cutter as a guide. Serge over the folded edge, being careful not to cut the fabric. Secure one end of the elastic by pinning or sewing it and pull up the elastic to complete the shirring.

For more controlled shirring, serge over *elastic thread* using a 4-thread stitch. Feed the elastic thread through the front hole and under the back of the presser foot. The elastic thread will be serged between the two needles, as for the filler cord, above. The shirring will be a little bulkier and will require more fabric because of the wider stitch, but it will remain more evenly distributed during wearing.

To serge-shirr with 1/8" *clear elastic*, adjust for a wide 3-thread stitch. Thread the elastic through the front hole and under the back of the presser foot. You will be serging over, and not through, the elastic. Anchor and draw up the shirring as for the elastic thread.

An optional shirring method is to serge through a strip of wider clear elastic, stretching the elastic as you serge. Use 1/4- or 3/8"-wide clear elastic. Adjust your serger for a medium stitch width and long stitch length. You will be serging through the elastic. Evenly section and mark the elastic and the fabric, leaving a section for starting before the first mark on the elastic. To begin, place the elastic under the foot and against the side of the cutter. Anchor it in back with your left hand to get started. Serge a few stitches on the elastic, then insert the folded fabric at the first mark. Serge, stretching the elastic to match the section marks, as shown. (Fig. 6-5)

Fig. 6-5: Shirr while serging by stretching clear elastic to meet presectioned markings.

 Special Tip: Use the *Superlock* elastic foot for the easiest application of shirring on clear elastic. Use 1/4"- or 3/8"-wide elastic and a long, wide stitch. Thread the elastic through the foot and out and under the back before attaching the foot to the machine. Before shirring your project, test the foot adjustment on a project scrap until you reach the desired amount of stretch.

Project:
Shirred Ponytail Tube

This simple yet pretty hair ornament is gathered with serge-shirred elastic. Rolled-edge stitching adds a decorative finish. Vary the fabric and measurements to whip up tubes and headbands for any occasion. (Fig. 6-6)

Fig. 6-6: *Shirred tubes dress up a hairstyle for special occasions or every day.*

Foot: Standard for elastic application; rolled edge for finishing
Plate: Standard for elastic application; rolled edge for finishing
Stitch: 3-thread
Stitch length: Medium (2.5 - 3mm) for elastic application; short (1 - 2mm) for rolled edge
Stitch width: Medium (2.8mm or 3.5mm) for elastic application; narrow for rolled edge
Thread: Matching or contrasting color
  Needle: All-purpose or serger
  Upper looper: All-purpose or serger for elastic application; decorative for rolled edge
  Lower looper: All-purpose or serger

Tension: Balanced for elastic application; rolled edge for finishing
Needle: Size 11/75
Fabric: One strip 3-1/2" wide by 18" long
Notions: 24" of elastic cord or 1-1/3 yards of elastic thread (used double-strand)

1. Allowing a 2" tail, thread the elastic cord (or two strands of elastic thread) through the rear hole and under the back of the presser foot. Serge several stitches over the elastic with a medium-width, balanced stitch.

2. Fold the fabric strip right sides together. Serge over the elastic on the folded fabric edge, being careful not to cut the fold of the fabric.

3. Secure one end of the elastic. Pull the opposite end to gather the fabric (to about 6" to 7" finished).

4. With the fabric ends flat and with the right sides of both ends together, straight-stitch the ends into a tube, back-stitching over the elastic to secure. (Fig. 6-7) Knot the elastic ends and trim.

Fig. 6-7: *After pulling the elastic to shirr, straight-stitch the ends to form a tube. Back-stitch over the elastic to secure.*

5. Fold the fabric wrong sides together. Finish the tube by serge-seaming with a rolled edge, overlapping the beginning stitching to finish.

Lesson 24.
Serger Lace

One of our favorite details for finishing dainty tucks on garment fronts and collars, serger lace also has interesting applications on numerous craft and accessory projects.

This lace is made by merely overlapping rows of balanced 3-thread serging. The appearance of serger lace can be varied by the thread used in the loopers and the number of rows of serging (more rows create a wider lace). Using buttonhole twist will give the look of a hand-crocheted edge. Lightweight thread creates a more delicate effect.

1. Adjust your serger for the longest, widest 3-thread stitch. Loosen all the tensions (or remove the thread from the tension controls) for the laciest stitch.

2. Serge one row of stitching to the fabric, allowing all but the needleline to hang off the edge. Leave at least a 4" thread chain at each end.

3. Overlap a second row of serging with the needle inside the overlocking loops of the first row of stitching. (Fig. 6-8)

Fig. 6-8: Overlap rows of 3-thread serging to form lace.

4. To make wider lace, continue overlapping rows of serging to the width desired. It may take a little practice to position the needle just inside the loops. If the needle misses stitching inside the loops, you will have a hole in the lace. In this case, simply find the shortest thread (the needle thread) and pull it. The loops will fall away from the previous stitching, and you can serge the row again.

5. If you want to ruffle the lace, serge several rows and gently stretch it parallel to the edge. (Fig. 6-9)

Fig. 6-9: Gently stretch the lace to ruffle it.

Stabilized lace

Easily make a perfect serged lace edge with water-soluble stabilizer as a base.

1. Serge-finish the fabric edge.

2. Cut a piece of stabilizer four times the finished width by the finished length of the lace you'll be making.

3. Adjust your serger for the longest, widest, and balanced 3-thread stitch. Loosen all the tensions to 0.

4. Place the stabilizer on the wrong side of the finished fabric, allowing it to extend 1/4" beyond the edge. Serge with the needleline just inside the loops of the previous stitching. (Fig. 6-10)

stabilizer

serge-finish edge

Fig. 6-10: Add stabilized lace to a fabric edge. Serge-finish the edge. Place water-soluble stabilizer underneath, extending 1/4" beyond the edge. Serge, catching the needleline inside the previous stitching. Fold the stabilizer and repeat for the desired width. Spray or soak to remove the stabilizer.

5. Fold the stabilizer to the right of the serging. Then refold the stabilizer back, leaving a stitch width of stabilizer to the right of the stitching, as shown.

6. Serge over the fold with the needleline just inside the loops of the previous stitching. Repeat for each additional row until the lace is the desired width.

7. Carefully spray or soak the lace in water to remove the stabilizer.

8. Allow the lace to air dry or dry it in the microwave on medium power, setting the timer for one-minute intervals and checking after each minute. When dry, it will have a starched feel. To soften it, carefully manipulate the lace with your fingers.

Make a stable lace trim following the same procedure. Begin by cutting the stabilizer following step 2 above and adjusting your serger following step 3. Serge-finish one long edge of the stabilizer, then follow steps 5 through 8 to complete the trim. (Fig. 6-11)

Fig. 6-11: Make stable lace trim by serging one edge of the stabilizer, folding it to the right and refolding to leave a stitch-width to the right. Serge the new fold with the needle just inside the previous stitch. Repeat for the width desired.

Serger lace tucks

Serger lace tucks are easier if you serge onto the fabric before cutting out the project. Begin by folding the fabric on the first tuck line. Serge-finish the edge with the needle about 1/8" inside the fold. Allow the loops to hang off the edge of the fabric. (Use a blindhem foot to ensure even stitching.) Continue folding and serging the tucks, using the presser foot to guide your stitching evenly. (Fig. 6-12) For wider lace tucks, serge another row of stitching inside the first row of loops. More delicate care may be required for this wider lace.

Fig. 6-12: Serge even lace tucks by guiding the presser-foot edge along the previous row.

Lacy fishline ruffles

To add a lace finish on the edge of fishline ruffles, apply the fishline according to the instructions in Lesson 7 (page 64). Serge the first row of lace with the needle just inside the rolled edge. Serge additional rows for wider lace.

Lace-trimmed wires

Serger lace also can be used to trim fine, flexible wires for craft projects. Cover the wire with a narrow rolled-edge stitch, guiding the wire under the presser foot between the needle and the cutter, *serging slowly*.

Change to the standard foot and plate and adjust your serger for a wide, long, and balanced 3-thread stitch. Serge over the covered wire, keeping it between the needle and the cutter, with the stitch loops hanging off the edge. Serge additional rows to make wider lace. Shape the lace-trimmed wire as desired and twist the ends together. (Fig. 6-13) Secure all the thread ends with seam sealant.

Fig. 6-13: Serge lace over covered wire and shape as desired.

Project:
Serger-Lace Flower

Make a delicate flower by adding rows of serger lace to a strip of bias tricot. After serge-gathering, apply stiffening agent to the flower to keep it fresh and fluffy. Vary the size of the flower or the type of thread used. Attach your finished sample to the padded picture frame completed in Lesson 18 (page 93). (Fig. 6-14)

Fig. 6-14: Make a delicate flower by gathering serger lace.

Foot: Standard
Plate: Standard
Stitch: 3-thread
Stitch length: Long
Stitch width: Widest
Thread:
    Needle: All-purpose or serger
    Upper looper: All-purpose or
      serger
    Lower looper: All-purpose or
      serger

Tension: Balanced
Needle: Size 11/75
Notions: 18" of 5/8"-wide *Seams Great* or other bias tricot; stiffening spray or dip, such as *Stiffy* or *TAC Spray Stiff*

1. Apply serger lace to one long edge of the bias tricot, following the instructions above. Begin with one row of stitching on the tricot, then add four more rows of stitching to complete the lace. (Fig. 6-15)

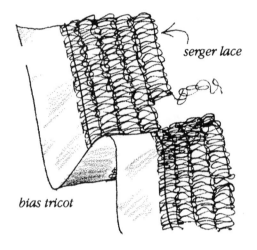

serger lace

bias tricot

Fig. 6-15: Serge four rows of lace on the edge of an 18" tricot strip.

2. Serge-gather the unfinished side of the tricot using the tension or differential-feed methods in Lesson 23 (page 111). If the edge does not gather tightly, pull the needle thread (the shortest thread) to gather it further.

3. Spray (or dip) the flower with stiffening solution, following the directions on the bottle.

4. Glue or hand-tack the finished flower to the padded picture frame, covering the joined ends of the piped binding.

Lesson 25. Decorative Flatlocking

In Lesson 3, we discussed basic flatlocking as it relates to flatlocked seams. Flatlocking also can be applied on folds, so it can be used as decorative detailing anywhere on a garment or project. Among its varied applications, we've seen flatlocking stitched at angles across the front of an embellished sweatshirt or added as a delicate accent on dressier cuffs and collars.

For the following techniques, unless otherwise specified, adjust your serger for basic flatlocking tensions and use either 2- or 3-thread flatlocking. (See page 48 for details.) Loosen the needle tension enough to allow the serging to pull flat after being stitched. Tighten the lower looper until it forms a straight line, and use decorative thread in the upper looper.

For most flatlocking, simply move the fabric fold to the left of the cutter about half of the stitch width. This also allows the stitches to hang off the edge for the flattest flatlocking. Use the *Superlock* blindhem foot to stitch evenly. Bring the fabric under the foot's guide (not in it) so that the fabric fold is positioned in the center of the stitching.

In addition to balanced 3-thread flatlocking, other novelty flatlocking effects can be achieved by changing tensions, stitch widths, and thread types.

Corded flatlocking

Flatlocking does not always require a wide stitch width. Narrow, satin-stitch flatlocking gives the appearance of cording or piping. For a more corded effect, use the right needle (on a 4-thread machine) and tighten the needle tension slightly to raise the stitch. (Fig. 6-16) Shorten the stitch

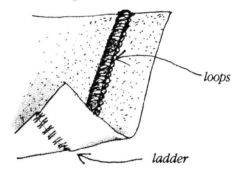

Fig. 6-16: *For corded flatlocking, tighten the needle tension.*

length for maximum thread coverage. A narrow ladder stitch will show from the underside. For the narrowest corded flatlocking, use the rolled-edge foot and plate.

Safety-stitch flatlocking

Flatlock with a wide 4-thread overedge stitch for safety-stitched flatlocking. Use a short- to medium-length, wide stitch and loosen both needle threads. (Fig. 6-17) On the

4-thread overedge stitch

Fig. 6-17: Loosen both needle tensions for safety-stitch flatlocking. With slightly tighter tension, a fold forms underneath loops.

underside, the ladder stitch will look just like the 3-thread flatlock. The loops on the top side will have an extra right needle-thread line showing. For accuracy, use the blindhem foot as a guide. Adjust to the widest setting, making sure both needles are serging on the fabric.

Safety-stitch flatlocking may not pull completely flat if you are unable to loosen your needle tensions enough. An option for this stitch is to create a raised fold underneath the flatlocked loops using a slightly tighter needle tension. (Fig. 6-17)

Balanced flatlocking

Basic 3-thread flatlocking can be adjusted so the looper tensions are balanced, with the upper and lower looper stitches overlocking in the center of the stitch. (Fig. 6-18) The

one color in upper looper

second color in lower looper

Fig. 6-18: Flatlocking with balanced looper tensions creates two-toned stitch.

needle tension remains loose so the stitch will lie flat. Use contrasting thread colors in the loopers for a multicolored stitch.

Mock hemstitching

For mock hemstitching, simply straight-stitch through a wide flatlocked stitch. For the ladder side out, flatlock with the right sides together. Pull the fabric flat. Top-stitch from the wrong side with monofilament nylon thread in the bobbin and thread that matches the fabric in the needle. (Fig. 6-19) The ladder stitches will automatically bunch together. With this stitch, the serger needle thread is the ladder thread that shows, so the decorative thread you use must be able to be threaded through the needle. Experiment with the stitch length for different effects.

Mock hemstitching also can be flatlocked with the looped side out. (Fig. 6-19) Use the decorative thread

ladder on right side   loops on right side

Fig. 6-19: *Straight-stitch either the looped or ladder side of flatlocking to create mock hemstitching.*

in the looper. Flatlock and then top-stitch from the ladder side with monofilament nylon thread in the bobbin and thread that matches the fabric in the needle.

Serge-fagoting

Fagoting is a decorative flatlock stitch used for fabric embellishment or seams when the area will not be subjected to much stress, such as the front of a blouse. Most often used in heirloom sewing on fine fabrics, fagoting is serged with the ladder side out. Use decorative thread in the needle. For inconspicuous loops (they may be seen from the top side after the edges are pulled apart), use monofilament nylon thread in the upper looper.

If you apply serge-fagoting to your garment fabric before cutting it out, establish a fagoting seamline and cut along it. Serge-finish the seam allowances and press them to the wrong side. Adjust for a long, wide flatlock stitch. With right sides together and the folds aligned, flatlock with the needle barely catching the edge of the fabric. Pull the stitching flat and press carefully. (Fig. 6-20)

Fig. 6-20: *For serge-fagoting, press the seam allowances back. Flatlock, barely catching the folds. Then pull the stitches flat.*

For further embellishment, thread 1/8"-wide ribbon through the ladder stitches. Securely top-stitch the seam allowances on both sides of the fagoting, using a decorative stitch on your sewing machine. Now center your pattern over the yardage and cut it out.

Project: Sampler Pin Cushion

Practice these new techniques by making rows of decorative flatlocking on this handy pin cushion. Select a soft woven fabric and tone-on-tone thread for a subtle effect. (Fig. 6-21)

Fig. 6-21: *Display decorative flatlocking options on a pretty pin cushion.*

Foot: Standard
Plate: Standard
Stitch: 3- and 4-thread
Stitch length: Short (1 - 2mm) for corded flatlocking, balanced flatlocking, and mock hemstitching; medium for safety-stitch; and long for fagoting
Stitch width: Narrow for corded; widest for all others
Thread: Same tone as fabric; monofilament nylon for bobbin
   Needle(s): All-purpose, serger, or rayon
   Upper looper: All-purpose, serger, or rayon
   Lower looper: All-purpose or serger; contrasting tone for balanced
Tension: Flatlock, unless otherwise indicated
Needle(s): Size 11/75
Fabric: 1/4 yard batiste, organdy, or broadcloth
Notions: 1/3 yard of 1/8"-wide satin ribbon—same tone as fabric and thread; polyester fiberfill for stuffing

1. Cut one 9" square from the fabric. Cut the square in half on the lengthwise grain.

2. On one long side of each piece, press 1/2" to the wrong side. With right sides together, apply fagoting. Pull the piece flat and weave the ribbon through the fagoted stitch. Decoratively top-stitch on both sides of the fagoting.

3. On both sides of the fagoting, with right sides together, serge a row of mock hemstitching a presser foot's width away from the fagoting. Top-stitch from the wrong side with monofilament nylon in the bobbin.

4. Serge a row of balanced flatlocking on either side of the mock hemstitching, using a contrasting thread color in the lower looper. Use the presser-foot width as a stitching guide.

5. On either side of the balanced flatlocking, serge a row of narrow corded flatlocking. Then, if your serger has a 4-thread overedge stitch, add rows of safety-stitch flatlocking.

6. Cut one 6" by 7" rectangle from the flatlocked fabric and two 6" by 7" rectangles from the unfinished fabric.

7. Using one of the plain rectangles as a backing for the flatlocked piece, place the right sides of the rectangles together. Serge-seam with a wide, medium length, and balanced 3- or 4-thread stitch. Leave an opening on one side to stuff the fiberfill.

8. Stuff the pin cushion and hand-tack the opening closed.

Lesson 26. Fringing

We see fringing on everything from scarves and garment edges to tablecloths and napkins. Using either flatlocking or balanced stitching, you can add a stable, decorative accent to the edge of any fringe. For fastest fringing, choose a fabric that ravels easily.

Flatlocked fringe

Choose balanced flatlocking or one of the other flatlocking options in Lesson 25.

1. Select the width of fringe desired and pull a thread to mark the lines—at least 1" from the edge.

2. Fold your fabric wrong sides together and flatlock over the fringe line with a short- to medium-length, medium-width stitch. Use a matching or contrasting thread color in both the upper looper and the needle.

3. Start at a corner where the marked lines intersect. Flatlock to the next intersection and (before turning) pull the previous stitching flat. (Fig. 6-22) Fold the next side, turn the fabric a quarter turn, and repeat for the remaining sides.

4. Secure the ends by weaving the thread chains under the stitching.

5. For easiest fringing, clip from the cut edge to (but not through) the stitching every 2". Fringe to the stitching line by pulling out the horizontal threads.

Fig. 6-22: For flatlocked fringe, serge on the fold between the intersecting lines. Pull the stitching flat, turn the square corner, and repeat for the adjoining side.

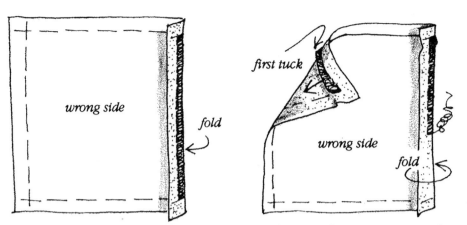

Fig. 6-23: *For tucked fringe, use a balanced stitch. Serge between the intersecting marks and fold the tuck toward the center. Repeat for the adjoining sides.*

Tucked fringe

For this edging option, serge a tuck and then top-stitch it down to the fabric next to the area to be fringed.

1. Put decorative thread in the upper looper and adjust for a short, medium to wide, and balanced 3-thread stitch.

2. Pull a thread 1-1/4" from the edges to mark the fringing lines.

3. Fold under 1-1/4" to the wrong side and, with the wrong side up, serge-finish along the fold to form a tuck. At the corner, serge to the intersection of the marked lines. Raise the presser foot, clear the stitches from the stitch finger manually or by pressing the tension-release lever, pull the fabric back behind the needle, and serge off. (Fig. 6-23)

4. Fold the serge-finished tuck away from the cut edge. Fold the adjoining edge along the marked line, in the same manner as for step 3. Clear the stitches from the stitch finger again and position the needle directly over the outside edge of the previous stitching. Begin by serging over the previous tuck, then continue serging the edge as in step 3.

5. Repeat steps 3 and 4 for the remaining edges to be fringed.

6. Press the finished tucks away from the edges. Hide the thread chains under the tucks and top-stitch to secure.

7. Clip the cut edges below the tucks every 2" and fringe by pulling out the horizontal threads.

Project: Fringed Triangle Scarf

This fashionable scarf is made from a folded square of challis. The double thickness gives a thick fringed edge, and the bias fold drapes softly at the neckline. Attach the corded frog closures made in Lesson 21 (page 107). Whether you wear the scarf with the frogs in front or at the shoulder, it will stay securely in place. (Fig. 6-24)

Fig. 6-24: Fringe two sides of a folded challis triangle. Secure with frog closures from Lesson 21.

Foot: Standard
Plate: Standard
Stitch: 3-thread
Stitch length: Medium (2.5mm - 3mm)
Stitch width: Medium to wide
Thread: Contrasting color
   Needle: All-purpose or serger
   Upper looper: Heavy rayon, such as *Decor 6* or pearl rayon
   Lower looper: All-purpose or serger
Tension: Balanced
Needle: Size 11/75
Fabric: One yard wool challis

1. Cut a 36" square of challis. On two adjoining sides, pull a thread or press-mark the fabric 1-1/4" from each side to mark the fringe lines.

2. Fold the scarf in half diagonally with the two marked fringe lines on top.

3. On one side, along the marked line, fold both layers of the fringe allowance 1-1/4" to the wrong side. Lightly press. Then turn the wrong side up and serge-finish the fold, stopping at the point where the two marked lines intersect. Raise the presser foot, clear the stitch finger, pull the remaining fabric behind the needle, and chain off.

4. Press the serged tuck toward the fabric, wrapping the thread chains underneath. Top-stitch to secure.

5. Repeat steps 3 and 4 for the other fringed side. Begin serge-finishing with the needle positioned exactly on the outer edge of the previous stitching at the point of the scarf. Serge to the end of the fabric and chain off.

6. On the two scarf points adjoining the folded edge, the fringe allowance and serged tuck will extend past the edge of the scarf. Fold the extension back and, to secure it, top-stitch across the tuck stitching. (Fig. 6-25)

Fig. 6-25: The fringe and tuck will extend past the folded edge of the scarf. Fold the end under and top-stitch.

7. Clip the fringe allowance every 2" and pull out the horizontal threads.

8. Hand-tack the frog closures made in Lesson 21 (page 107) to the unfringed scarf edges. Position them 8" and 11" from the bottom of the fringe. Attach the frogs so the edges of the scarf meet, but don't overlap, under the frogs.

Lesson 27.
Serging over Trim

If a decorative thread, yarn, or ribbon is too bulky (or not flexible enough) to thread through your loopers, you have the option of serging over it. In order to fully cover a trim with serging, it must be narrow enough to fit between the needle and the cutter. The upper looper also must be able to clear the trim without catching so the stitches will form evenly.

To serge over decorative trim, adjust for a stitch width wide enough to cover the trim. The length of the stitch will depend on how much of the trim you want to expose. Start with a medium stitch length for testing. Use a balanced 3-thread stitch or a 3-thread flatlock. Use monofilament nylon or matching serger thread in the upper looper to emphasize the trim.

Place the trim under the back and flat over the front of the presser foot, to guide it between the needle and the cutters. Allow several inches of trim to extend behind the foot for easy starting.

Special Tip: Use the *Superlock* pearl/sequin foot to help serge over trim easily. (Fig. 6-26) Place the trim along the right edge of the foot so it rests in the front guide and feeds under the back guide. When trimming an edge, bring

Fig. 6-26: Serge the trim to the fabric with a pearl/sequin foot.

the fabric completely under the foot to the cutter. When flatlocking on a fold, guide the fabric under the foot's fabric guide away from the cutter so the trim and stitching fall half on and half off the fabric; this allows the finished flatlocking to pull flat.

For the easiest feeding, begin serging over the trim for several stitches with no fabric underneath. Then insert the fabric under the foot and serge slowly. Be careful not to stitch through the trim or cut it with the cutter. Especially if it's bulky, you may need to hold the trim taut to guide it out from under the back of the foot.

Flatlocking over ribbon

Try flatlocking over a ribbon to cover a seam. The ribbon should be narrow enough to be serged over without cutting or stitching through it. The 1/8"-wide ribbon works with a 5mm stitch width. Use the 1/16"-wide ribbon for a narrower 3-thread stitch.

1. Serge-seam the fabric with right sides together.

2. Apply the ribbon following the instructions for flatlocking over trim on page 126.

3. Fold the fabric on the seamline, wrong sides together. Raise the presser foot and put the fabric halfway under the ribbon. Flatlock through all layers, with the stitches just covering the ribbon edges. (Fig. 6-27)

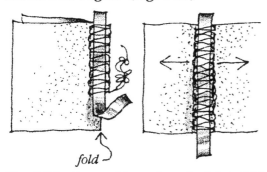

Fig. 6-27: Center ribbon along the fabric fold before flatlocking. The stitches will hang off the edge. Pull flat.

4. Pull the stitching flat and the ribbon will cover the seamline.

Flatlocking over lace and ribbon

Another decorative technique is to center a layer of double-edged lace over the seamline on the right side of the fabric. Then fold the lace and the fabric along the seamline and flatlock the ribbon on top (through all layers) using the method for flatlocking over ribbon, opposite. (Fig. 6-28)

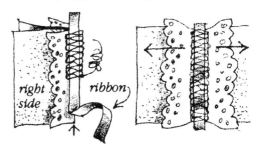

Fig. 6-28: Flatlock to attach a layer of ribbon and lace to fabric.

Flatlocking over yarn

Flatlocking over yarn with monofilament nylon thread appears to leave the yarn floating on the fabric surface.

1. Fold the fabric right sides together with the yarn inside the fold. (Fig. 6-29)

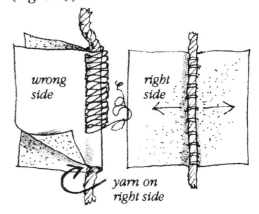

Fig. 6-29: Flatlock over decorative yarn from the wrong side. Only the ladder stitch shows on the right side.

2. Thread monofilament nylon in the needle and matching all-purpose or serger thread in the looper(s).

3. Serge the fold with a wide, long flatlock stitch.

4. Pull the fold flat. From the right side, the yarn floats on the surface, held invisibly by the monofilament.

 Special Tip: If you have difficulty catching the yarn in the fold, baste it with a zigzag stitch to hold it in place for the flatlocking. Use monofilament nylon thread in the needle for invisible zigzag basting.

Project: Heart-shaped Jewelry Holder

This feminine jewelry holder is decoratively finished by flatlocking over ribbon. Covered hooks hold necklaces tangle-free. (Fig. 6-30)

Fig. 6-30: A pillowed jewelry holder keeps bracelets and necklaces tangle-free.

Foot: Pearl/sequin foot for ribbon application; standard for serge-seaming
Plate: Standard
Stitch: 3-thread for flatlocking; 3- or 4-thread for serge-seaming
Stitch length: Medium to long (2.5 - 5mm) for flatlocking; medium (2.5 - 3mm) for serge-seaming
Stitch width: Widest (4mm or 5mm)
Thread: Matching color
    Needle(s): All-purpose or serger
    Upper looper: Monofilament nylon for flatlocking; all-purpose or serger for serge-seaming
    Lower looper: All-purpose or serger
Tension: Flatlocking for ribbon application; balanced for serge-seaming
Needle(s): Size 11/75
Fabric: 1/4 yard batiste; 1/4 yard lace yardage (will make two holders)
Notions: 2 yards 1/8"-wide satin ribbon (1/16"-wide for narrower stitch widths); 5 large covered hooks (used on heavy coats); one yard 3/4"-wide ruffled lace; fiberfill for stuffing

1. Using the pattern grid (Fig. 6-31), cut one lace and two fabric heart pieces.

2. With the wrong sides of the lace together, flatlock four strips of ribbon to the lace heart piece, as shown on the pattern grid.

3. Change to the standard presser foot and adjust for a balanced stitch. Layer one fabric heart under the lace

Fig. 6-31: Jewelry holder pattern, with ribbon and hook placement marked.

heart. Fold 1/2" of the ruffled lace to the wrong side. Beginning at the lower point, place the right side of the ruffled lace against the right side of the two heart layers (lace heart on top). Serge the lace to the heart, pulling the edge out straight at the inside corner on the top of the heart. Overlap the beginning lace at the point.

4. With the ruffled lace sandwiched between, place the remaining fabric heart right sides together with the lace heart. Beginning at the lower point, serge-seam, leaving a 3" opening for the stuffing.

5. Turn the heart right side out and stuff with fiberfill. Hand-tack the opening closed.

6. Hand-tack a bow and hanging loop at the top and five hooks on the front, as in the finished view on page 128.

Lesson 28. Sequin, Bead, and Pearl Application

Strands of colorful beads, elegant pearls, and shiny sequins can be serged to edges or anywhere else on your garment or project. Use them for bridalwear, holiday glitz, or just for fun.

Applying beads and pearls

Beaded trims (available at craft and fabric stores or through mail order) can be applied with a flatlock, rolled edge, or even a balanced stitch. The beads must be small enough to fit between the needle and cutter and for the upper looper to pass over them. Purchase enough yardage for thorough testing before application.

Beads or sequins may be applied by removing the presser foot and guiding them manually between the needle and the cutter. However, the *Superlock* pearl/sequin foot simplifies the application for beads or sequins up to a 1/4" width.

1. If your machine has two needles, remove the right one.

2. Adjust for a stitch slightly longer and wider than the beads you are applying.

3. Use monofilament nylon thread in the upper looper and matching all-purpose or serger thread in the needle and lower looper.

4. If you are attaching the beads to a fold, adjust for a flatlock stitch (see page 48) using the standard plate and the pearl/sequin foot. If you are attaching the beads to an edge, adjust for a rolled edge using the rolled-edge plate and the pearl/sequin foot.

5. Place the bead strand along the right side of the foot so it rests in the front guide and feeds under the back one. Allow 2 - 3" to extend beyond the back of the foot. (Fig. 6-32)

Fig. 6-32: Easily serge over beaded trim using the pearl/sequin foot.

6. Serge slowly over several inches of beading before inserting the fabric. Then guide the fabric fold or edge (bead stitching line) under (not in) the guide on the front of the foot. Determine how far from the cutter you'll guide the fabric during your testing before flatlocking beads to your project.

If you're guiding beads manually without the foot, remember to allow the beads and stitches to hang off the edge when using a flatlock stitch.

To serge off, cut the trim and carefully serge over the trim end. If necessary, use seam sealant to secure the beads before cutting.

Beaded piping

To make a piping strip of beads or pearls, serge the strands to a folded 1-1/4"-wide bias strip of tricot or other lightweight fabric.

Applying sequins

To serge over sequin trim, the sequins must be narrow enough for the looper thread to lock over them or no wider than 1/4" for application with the pearl foot (see applying beads and pearls). Place the trim so that the sequins overlap away from the presser foot. (Fig. 6-33) Serge

Fig. 6-33: Overlap sequin trim away from the presser foot.

over the sequin trim with a long stitch length, being careful to avoid hitting the needle or cutter. Use monofilament nylon thread or matching thread in the upper looper. After serging, slip the upper looper threads between the sequins so no thread is visible.

Project: Bead-edged Flower

A strand of pearl beading can be applied to a folded edge of organza to create an elegant flower accessory.

Attach it to a pin or hair comb, or use it to adorn the evening bag you'll make in Lesson 36. (Fig. 6-34)

Fig. 6-34: Beaded trim dresses up the edges of an organza flower.

Foot: Pearl/sequin for bead application; standard for serge-gathering
Plate: Rolled edge for bead application; standard for serge-gathering
Stitch: 3-thread for bead application and serge-gathering
Stitch length: Medium (2.5 - 3mm) —slightly longer than the individual bead
Stitch width: Narrow (1.8mm or 2mm) to cover the bead; wide (4mm or 5mm) for serge-gathering
Thread: Matching color
  Needle: All-purpose or serger
  Upper looper: Monofilament nylon, all-purpose, or serger
  Lower looper: All-purpose or serger
Tension: Rolled edge for bead application; balanced for serge-gathering

Needle: Size 11/75
Fabric: 5" of organza or georgette (45" wide)
Notions: 1-1/2 yards of pearl beading

1. Fold the fabric strip in half lengthwise. Serge the pearl beading to the folded edge using the pearl foot and a rolled-edge stitch.

2. Change to the standard plate and foot. Adjust your serger for serge-gathering, using one of the techniques in Lesson 23 (page 110). With the presser foot raised, begin the gathering by carefully serging over the pearls at one end. Lower the presser foot and taper to the cut edges, finishing the edges. (Fig. 6-35) Taper off at the other end, raising the presser foot as you serge over the pearls.

Fig. 6-35: Taper the strip ends while serge-gathering. Raise the foot when serging over the pearls.

3. If you want more gathering, pull on the needle thread (the shortest thread in the chain). Shape the strip into a flower and hand-tack the gathered edges together.

Lesson 29.
Serge-Couching

Couching braid (for embellishing fabric with curved or looped designs) can be created on your serger. Create the braid by serging over a filler, such as strands of heavier thread or cord, using a rolled-edge stitch. Or make the puffed serged braid featured in Lesson 21 (page 105) by serging over tubes of bias fabric or thick yarn.

Use heavier decorative thread in the upper looper and matching all-purpose or serger thread in the needle and lower looper. Thread the filler through the presser foot using the technique in Lesson 4 (page 54). Or use the pearl foot for heavier filler up to 1/4" wide (see serging over trim, page 126).

For a flatter couching braid, use a lighter-weight filler or fewer filler threads. Or if you use heavy thread in the upper looper, you may choose not to have a filler at all. Adjust your serger for a short, narrow, and balanced 3-thread stitch. Tighten the lower looper slightly. The lower looper thread should not show, and any filler should be covered entirely by the upper looper thread.

Sew couching braid to your fabric by straight-stitching through it, zigzag-

ging over it, or stitching beside it with a sewing machine blindhem stitch. Straight-stitching works best on flatter braid. You may need to zigzag over a thicker braid. (Fig. 6-36) Use monofilament nylon or matching thread in the needle.

Fig. 6-36: *Straight-stitch flatter couching braid, zigzag over thicker braid.*

To apply couching directly with your serger, use a balanced or flatlock stitch. This application requires straighter design lines, but loops can be formed in the couching braid to add interest. The loops are later glued, hand-tacked, straight-stitched, or zigzagged down. (Fig. 6-37) Or you may choose to thread a bead on the loop as you work, before securing the second side. If so, leave the loop loose.

For easier couching application, use a fusible thread in the lower looper when making the braid. Loosen the lower looper tension to allow more coverage for the fusible thread. Fuse the braid to your fabric to complete the couching. Or for more durability after fusing, zigzag over the braid.

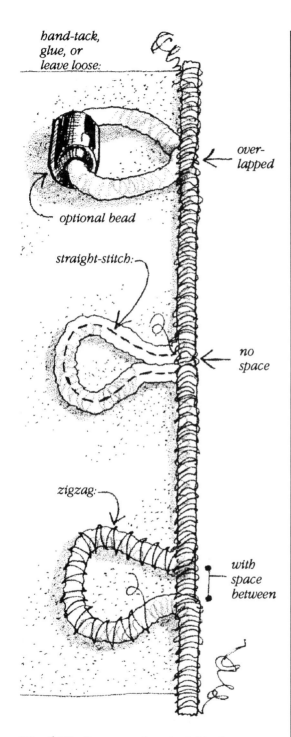

hand-tack, glue, or leave loose:

optional bead

over-lapped

straight-stitch:

no space

zigzag:

with space between

Fig. 6-37: *Serge-couch a straight edge, leaving loops. Variations add interest.*

Project: Couched Tree Ornament

Little couched pillows add a festive touch to any Christmas tree. They're made quickly with rolled-edge finishing and serged couching braid. Vary the fabric, thread color, and couching design to individualize each ornament. (Fig. 6-38)

Fig. 6-38: *Couching personalizes an easy Christmas ornament.*

Foot: Standard for braid; rolled edge for serge-seaming
Plate: Standard for braid; rolled edge for serge-seaming
Stitch: 3-thread
Stitch length: Short (1 - 2mm)
Stitch width: Narrow (1.8mm or 2mm)
Thread: Contrasting color
   Needle: Matching
   Upper looper: Woolly nylon
   Lower looper: Fusible for braid; woolly or monofilament nylon for rolled-edge serge-seaming

Tension: Balanced for braid; rolled edge for serge-seaming
Needle: Size 11/75 (14/90 if using fusible thread)
Fabric: 1/6 yard woven fabric
Notions: Heavy filler thread (crochet or pearl cotton); fiberfill for stuffing

1. Cut two 4" fabric squares on the bias grain.

2. With an air-erasable marker, draw a couching design on both squares. Use initials or simple designs such as bells, stars, or Christmas trees. (Use cookie cutters for other shapes.)

3. With a narrow, balanced stitch and your serger threaded according to the specifications above, serge over four strands of filler to create one yard of braid. (Thread the filler through the rear hole on the standard presser foot.)

4. Fuse the braid over the designs on the squares, tucking the ends underneath. Zigzag over the braid with monofilament nylon thread.

5. Change to the rolled-edge plate (still using the standard foot) and adjust your serger for a rolled edge. Serge over two strands of the filler (threaded through the rear presser-foot hole), making a 6" chain.

6. Place the two squares wrong sides together, making certain the designs are going in the same direction.

7. Change to the rolled-edge foot and serge-seam three edges with a rolled edge. Stuff the pillow and complete by serge-seaming the final edge.

8. Form a hanging loop from the filler chain (step 5) and hand-tack it to the upper corner of the ornament.

7. Decorative Serged Closures

Although we have steered away from construction techniques in this book, this chapter is an exception. Decorative closures can be an important design element in your serging projects. For example, a colorful top-stitched zipper down the front of a top or pretty serge-bound buttonholes to match your jacket's edge-finishing provide an outstanding ornamental feature on your garment. Before discussing decorative closures, we will first outline the techniques for applying them. None are very complicated, and a few are actually simple.

Lesson 30. Lapped and Top-stitched Zippers

Zippers can be applied to garments and craft projects using several methods. The simplest application involves serge-finishing both fabric edges with a narrow decorative finish and top-stitching them single-layer to the right side of the zipper tape. This sporty technique leaves the zipper teeth exposed. Colorful zippers and a variety of thread choices lend a wide range of combinations.

Experiment with different edge finishes in Chapter 4. Adjust for a short, satin-stitch length for best thread coverage. Test first, though, because too short a stitch can cause an edge to stretch out.

For more durable edges, especially on lightweight or knit fabrics, press under the seam allowance and serge-finish on the fold. Add 1/2" allowances if there are none, press them under, and serge-finish.

Follow these simple steps for a lapped and top-stitched zipper:

1. With decorative thread in the upper looper, serge-finish the edges to be zipped. Serge from the right side, directly on the seamlines or over the fold.

2. Place the serge-finished edges on the top side of the zipper tape, next to the teeth.

3. Top-stitch with a straight-stitch along the needleline of the serging. (Fig. 7-1)

top-stitching

Fig. 7-1: *Top-stitch the lapped zipper next to the needleline of the decorative serging.*

The lapped and top-stitched zipper application is most often used when both ends of the zipper will be crossed and anchored by an intersecting seam.

Project: Serged Pencil Case

Fig. 7-2: *A sporty pencil case features a colorful lapped and top-stitched zipper.*

This zippered pencil case is a quick and easy project for your favorite student. Select fabrics and decorative edging to suit any taste. (Fig. 7-2)

Foot: Standard
Plate: Standard
Stitch: 3-thread for decorative; 3- or 4-thread for serge-seaming
Stitch length: Short (1 - 2mm) for decorative; medium (2.5 - 3mm) for serge-seaming
Stitch width: Medium (2.8mm or 3.5mm) for decorative; wide (4mm or 5mm) for serge-seaming
Thread: Contrasting color for decorative; matching color for serge-seaming
Needle(s): All-purpose or serger
Upper looper: Cotton crochet for decorative; all-purpose or serger for serge-seaming
Lower looper: All-purpose or serger
Tension: Balanced
Needle(s): Size 14/90
Fabric: 1/6 yard denim (make two cases from 45"-wide fabric)
Notions: One 9" zipper in contrasting color

1. Cut two 10" by 5" rectangles from the denim. Cut one rectangle lengthwise into two pieces, one 10" by 1-1/2" and the other 10" by 3-1/2".

2. Adjust your serger for decorative edging. Serge-finish one long edge of each of the narrower rectangles, trimming slightly.

3. Bartack the zipper tape together next to the upper zipper stop with a short zigzag stitch.

4. Center one decorative edge over the right side of the zipper tape. Top-stitch over the needleline of the decorative stitching. Repeat for the other side.

5. Open the zipper and place the two rectangles wrong sides together. The zippered half will be slightly wider than the plain half. Serge-seam all four sides, trimming off the extra fabric. When serging over both ends of the zipper, serge slowly and guide your needle right next to the zipper stops. Turn the case right side out through the zipper opening.

Lesson 31. Zipped Double-bound Edge

This decorative lapped zipper application uses a wide double-bound edge to cover the zipper teeth. Like the lapped and top-stitched zipper, the zipped double-bound edge is most often used when both zipper ends will later be intersected by a seam. The zipper pull and teeth will be neatly hidden.

For this application, use a wide 4mm or 5mm stitch. Cut any edge that will be double-bound 5/8" wider than your pattern. The extra allowance is necessary for the edge-finishing technique.

1. Place the zipper face down on the right side of the seamline, matching the zipper tape to the cut edge.

2. Adjust the serger for a medium-width, medium-length stitch. Serge the zipper to the seam allowance, as shown. (Fig. 7-3) Do not trim the

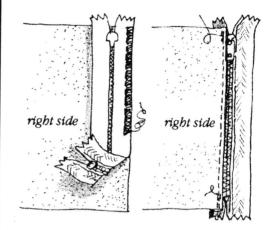

right side   *right side*

Fig. 7-3: *Serge the zipper to the right side of the fabric. Fold back the allowance and top-stitch.*

zipper tape. Hold the zipper and fabric taut to prevent the presser foot from slipping off the zipper teeth.

3. With the zipper right side up, form a fold in the seam allowance, close to the zipper teeth. Top-stitch the fold to the zipper tape.

4. Finish the fabric for the opposite side of the zipper with a double-bound edge (page 82).

5. Lap the double-bound edge over the zipper teeth and top-stitch in place. If your bound edge is a full 1/2" or more, you may choose to top-stitch on the center needleline. If the binding is narrower, top-stitch over the original top-stitching line.

Project: Dressed-up Cosmetic Bag

A wide double-bound edge hides the zipper on this quilted cosmetic bag. Show off your serging skills and please those on your gift list at the same time. (Fig. 7-4)

Fig. 7-4: A double-bound edge hides the zipper on a quilted cosmetic bag.

Foot: Standard
Plate: Standard
Stitch: 3-thread for decorative and zipper seaming; 3- or 4-thread for serge-seaming
Stitch length: Short (1 - 2mm) for decorative; medium (2.5 - 3mm) for serge-seaming
Stitch width: Wide (4mm or 5mm) for decorative and serge-seaming; medium (2.8mm or 3.5mm) for zipper seaming
Thread: Contrasting color for decorative; matching color for serge-seaming
Needle(s): All-purpose or serger

Upper looper: Two colors of woolly nylon for decorative; all-purpose or serger for serge-seaming
Lower looper: Fusible, all-purpose, or serger for decorative; all-purpose or serger for serge-seaming
Tension: Balanced
Needle(s): Size 11/75
Fabric: 1/3 yard quilted fabric (45"-wide fabric makes five bags)
Notions: One zipper 9" or longer; 6" of 1/4"-wide ribbon

1. Cut an 8" by 12" rectangle from the fabric.

2. Center the right side of the zipper on the right side of one short end of the fabric rectangle, matching the zipper tape to the cut edge. With a narrow stitch width, serge the zipper to the seam allowance.

3. On the other short end, press 3/4" to the wrong side. With decorative thread in the upper looper, serge-finish the fold from the wrong side. Carefully press the serged fold to the right side and top-stitch next to the overlocked loops. (See instructions for a double-bound edge, page 82.)

4. Fold the remaining fabric edge to the wrong side the same width as your previous decorative stitching. Serge over the fold with a contrasting thread color in the upper looper. Keep the needle right on the needleline of the previous stitching.

5. Lap the decorative edge over the unfinished side of the zipper so that the middle of the binding is next to the zipper teeth. With the zipper closed, top-stitch on top of the previous needleline, securing the decorative edge to the zipper tape. (Fig. 7-5)

Fig. 7-5: Top-stitch the decorative binding to the right side of the zipper tape.

6. Open the zipper and turn the bag inside out. Fold so the zipper is approximately 1-1/2" from the upper edge. Serge-seam the sides of the bag, slowly serging over the zipper tape. (Fig. 7-6)

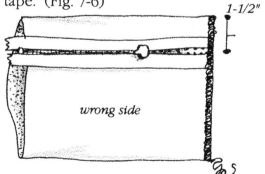

1-1/2"

wrong side

Fig. 7-6: Serge-seam the bag sides from the wrong side.

7. Turn the bag right side out. Knot the ribbon through the zipper pull.

Lesson 32. Serge-picked Zippers

This nifty (yet more complicated) zipper application produces results similar to a hand-picked zipper. Try both the centered and lapped methods in your fashion garments, from tailored to dressy. In addition to the decorative hand-picked look, the zipper is securely sewn to the seam allowance and all edges are neatly serge-finished. (Fig. 7-7)

Centered   *Lapped*

Fig. 7-7: Serge-picked zippers give a decorative, hand-picked appearance.

For a serge-picked zipper, adjust your serger to its longest-length, balanced 3-thread stitch. Follow the same procedures as when folding for a conventionally sewn blindhem. The needle of the serged stitch should barely catch the fold of the fabric. Stitches will be visible from the right side, but with matching thread they will appear hand-picked.

Special Tip: We found that practicing the serged blindhem technique before applying the zipper is the key to a professionally applied serge-picked zipper.

Buy a zipper that is at least 1" longer than the garment opening. The excess zipper will be cut off at the top. For both application methods, machine baste the opening closed. Press the seam allowances open.

Centered application

1. Place the zipper face down on the basted seam with the teeth directly on the seamline. Machine baste the zipper to the seam allowance, as shown, ending at the lower zipper stop. (Fig. 7-8)

Fig. 7-8: Machine baste the zipper to the seam allowances.

2. Repeat step 1, basting the zipper to the other seam allowance.

3. With the wrong side of the zipper down, fold the fabric exactly 1/4" away from the seamline, as shown. (Fig. 7-9) Serge-pick the zipper,

Fig. 7-9: Fold the fabric back, leaving 1/4" between the seam and foldline. Serge, barely catching the needle in the fold.

ending even with or above the lower zipper stop, making sure the seam allowance is folded exactly 1/4". Barely catch the needle in the fold of the fabric. The zipper tape and seam allowance will be trimmed slightly. Repeat for the other side of the zipper, starting even with or above the lower stop.

Special Tip: Use a *Superlock* blindhem foot for accuracy and ease when serge-picking. Adjust the foot so the needle barely catches in the fabric fold.

4. Pull the garment or project flat and press carefully.

5. To complete the bottom edge of the zipper, fold the fabric back from the lower edge of the zipper, as shown. (Fig. 7-10) With chalk or a

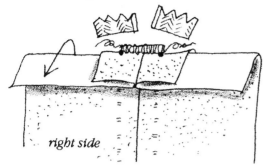

right side

Fig. 7-10: *Fold the fabric back at the bottom of the zipper. Trim the zipper tape. Mark and serge-pick the fabric between the needlelines.*

marking pen, mark the needlelines on the fold, as shown. Trim the zipper tape to 1/4". Beginning and ending exactly on the markings, serge-pick the lower edge. Use seam sealant to secure the ends of the serging.

6. Pull the garment flat and press carefully. Remove the machine basting from the seamline.

Lapped application

1. Place the zipper face down on the basted seam with the teeth directly over the seamline.

2. Adjust the serger for a narrow, medium-length stitch. Serge the zipper to the seam allowance, beginning at the lower zipper stop. (Fig. 7-11) Do not trim the zipper tape. Hold the zipper and fabric taut to prevent the presser foot from slipping off the zipper teeth.

wrong side

Fig. 7-11: *Center the zipper over the seamline. Beginning at the lower zipper stop, serge the zipper to the right seam allowance.*

3. With the zipper right side up, form a fold in the seam allowance, close to the zipper teeth. Top-stitch the fold to the zipper tape, as shown. (Fig. 7-12)

wrong side

Fig. 7-12: *With the zipper face up, fold the seam allowance close to the teeth. Top-stitch the fold.*

4. With the wrong side of the zipper down, machine baste the other side of the zipper tape to the seam allowance, beginning even with or above the lower zipper stop.

5. With the wrong side of the zipper still down, fold the fabric exactly 3/8" away from the seamline. (Fig. 7-13) Serge-pick one side as in step 3 of the centered application, beginning even with or above the lower zipper stop.

Fig. 7-13: Fold the fabric back 3/8". Serge, barely catching the needle in the fold.

6. Fold the garment back at the bottom of the zipper. Mark, trim, serge-pick, and complete the application as in steps 5 and 6 of the centered method.

Project: Tailored Garment Bag

Although a serge-picked zipper is most often seen in our finest garments, it works equally well for other projects like this sophisticated gar-

ment bag. Everyone will think your tailor finished it by hand. (Fig. 7-14)

Fig. 7-14: Make a tailored garment bag with a centered serge-picked zipper.

Foot: Blindhem for serge-picking; standard for serge-seaming
Plate: Standard
Stitch: 3-thread for serge-picking; 3- or 4-thread for serge-seaming
Stitch length: Longest (5mm) for serge-picking; medium (2.5 - 3mm) for serge-seaming
Stitch width: Wide (4mm or 5mm)
Thread: Matching or contrasting color for serge-picking; matching for serge-seaming
Needle(s): All-purpose or serger
Upper looper: All-purpose or serger
Lower looper: All-purpose or serger
Tension: Balanced
Needle(s): Size 11/75

Fabric: 1-1/2 yard woven fabric—
at least 54" wide

Notions: 42" zipper with one zipper
pull (purchase from upholstery
supply stores or by the yard from
mail-order sources)

1. Make the pattern for the back of
the garment bag by tracing around a
plastic hanger at the top of the bag.
Extend the pattern 2" on both sides
and 50" in length. Add 1/2" seam
allowances to all sides, then curve out
the top for the hanger opening.
(Fig. 7-15)

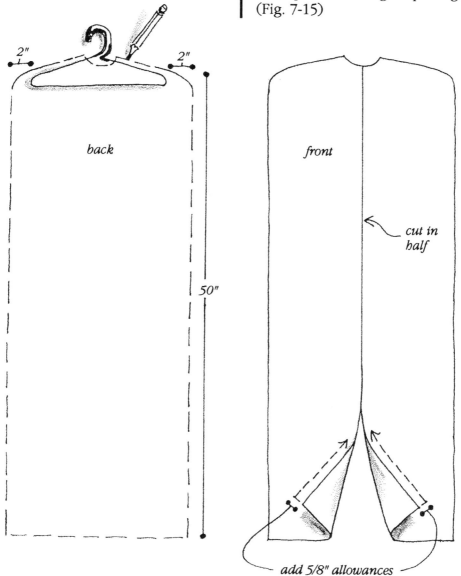

Fig. 7-15: *For the pattern back, trace around the top of a hanger. Add 2" at each side and extend the sides 50". For the front, trace the back and add center seam allowances.*

2. For the front pattern piece, trace the back and cut it in half lengthwise (for the center front opening). Add 5/8" seam allowances to the center front of both pieces.

3. Cut out the back and the two front pieces.

4. Place the front pieces right sides together. Starting at the top of the bag, straight-stitch the seamline for 2". Back-stitch and lengthen your stitch for machine basting. Continue along the seamline, basting to within 8" of the bottom edge. Switch to a regular straight-stitch. Back-stitch and complete the seam.

5. Place the zipper pull on the upper edge of the zipper and bartack 1-1/2" from the top of the zipper tape, making sure the pull is below the bartack.

6. Place the zipper face down on the basted seam, with the teeth directly on the seamline and the top edge of the zipper tape 1/2" from the top edge of the bag. Starting at the top of the zipper tape, machine baste the center of the zipper tape to the seam allowance on each side, ending 1" from the bottom of the zipper.

7. With the wrong side of the zipper down, fold 1/4" away from the seamline on one side and serge-pick the zipper, barely catching the needle in the fold of the fabric. (Refer back to Fig. 7-9, page 140.) Repeat for the other side of the zipper.

N **Note:** If the cutter does not trim the zipper tape smoothly, you will need to pretrim it before serge-picking.

8. Pull the bag flat and press carefully. Remove the basting threads.

9. Finish the lower part of the zipper by folding back the bag to the end of the zipper stitching. Trim the zipper to 1/4" and serge-pick between the two needlelines.

10. Serge-finish the top opening edge and the seam allowances below the zipper. Turn the top edge 1/4" to the wrong side and top-stitch to finish.

11. Open the zipper about 12". With right sides together, serge-seam the bottom edge of the bag. Then serge-seam both side seams of the bag. Weave the thread chains back through the serging. Turn the bag right side out through the zipper opening and tie a ribbon or cord to the zipper pull.

Lesson 33. Serge-bound Buttonholes

Buttonholes can be the bane of a sewing project, especially bound buttonholes with their complex and exacting procedure. But with your serger, decorative bound buttonholes are fast and easy. You can also use this technique for decorative welt pockets. Both can complement other decorative serging details on your garment or project.

1. Accurately mark the buttonhole placements on the wrong side of the fabric and on the facing.

2. With pinking shears cut rectangles of lightweight nonwoven fusible interfacing for each buttonhole in the fabric and the facing. The rectangles should be 2" wide and 1" longer than the buttonholes. Place the rectangles, resin side up, over the buttonhole positions on the right side of the fabric and facing.

3. From the wrong side of the fabric, straight-stitch the buttonhole rectangle markings. (Fig. 7-16)

Fig. 7-16: Straight-stitch the buttonhole rectangles from the wrong side, using the markings as a guide.

4. Cut the buttonholes open, clipping to the corners. Carefully turn the interfacing through to the wrong side. Working with the long edges first, finger-press, then fuse, using the tip of your iron.

5. Cut rectangles of paper-backed fusible web 1" wide by 1" longer than the buttonholes. Center them over the wrong side of the buttonhole openings with the web side down. Fuse,

remove the paper backings, then trim the web out of the openings. (Fig. 7-17)

Fig. 7-17: Pull the interfacing to the wrong side of the garment. Finger-press and fuse. Center the transfer web over the opening and press lightly.

6. To make the buttonhole lips, cut a 1"-wide strip of fabric twice the length of each buttonhole plus 2". Fold the strips in half lengthwise with wrong sides together. Serge-finish the folds with a satin length, balanced 3-thread or rolled-edge stitch. This serging is decorative, so test for the most attractive type and width of stitch for your fabric and pattern. Test different thread types as well.

7. Cut each strip in half and butt the serged edges together. Bartack them together at each end to form the buttonhole lips. The bartacks should not show in the finished buttonholes.

8. From the right side, center the buttonhole openings over the right side of the lips and fuse them in place,

using a press cloth to prevent shine.
(Fig. 7-18)

right side

Fig. 7-18: *Center the buttonhole over the lips. Fuse them in place and top-stitch.*

9. Top-stitch around the boxes, just outside the edges.

10. Fuse the facing to the back side of the buttonholes.

Project: Three-Button Belt

Easy serge-bound buttonholes provide the decorative detail on this *Ultrasuede* belt. It's adjustable by using one, two, or all three buttonholes. (Fig. 7-19)

Fig. 7-19: *This adjustable belt has three serge-bound buttonholes.*

Foot: Standard
Plate: Standard or rolled edge
Stitch: 3-thread
Stitch length: Short (1 - 2mm)
Stitch width: Narrow (1.8mm or 2mm) to medium (2.8mm or 3.5mm)
Thread: Contrasting color
    Needle: All-purpose or serger
    Upper looper: Woolly nylon
    Lower looper: Woolly nylon
Tension: Balanced
Needle: Size 11/75
Fabric: 34" by 4" strip *Ultrasuede* for belt (or adjust for your waist measurement plus 7"—see note below); 12" by 1" strip lightweight broadcloth or other woven for buttonhole lips
Notions: 2" by 34" (see note below) stiff fusible interfacing for belt backing; 16" by 2" strip lightweight nonwoven fusible interfacing for buttonholes; 16" by 1" strip paper-backed fusible web for six buttonhole windows; three 1" buttons

N **Note:** The belt measurements fit a size 27" to 32-1/2" waist. To alter, add to or subtract from the length of both the *Ultrasuede* strip and the stiff fusible interfacing. Use your waist measurement plus 7".

1. Cut the long strip of *Ultrasuede* in half lengthwise. Interface one strip for the top of the belt.

2. Starting 1/2" from one end, mark three 1-1/4" horizontal buttonholes 1-1/2" apart on the wrong side of each strip.

3. Place a 2-1/4" by 2" rectangle of fusible interfacing over the right side of each buttonhole with the resin side up. From the wrong side, straight-stitch buttonhole rectangles over the markings.

4. Cut the buttonholes open, clipping to the corners. Turn the interfacing to the wrong side, finger-pressing, then fusing.

5. Cut three 2-1/4" by 1" rectangles of transfer web. Center and fuse them over the buttonholes. Remove the paper backings and trim out the openings.

6. Fold the strip of broadcloth in half lengthwise and serge-finish the edge with a narrow satin stitch.

7. Cut six 2" sections from the serged strip. Form three sets of buttonhole lips by butting the serged edges together and bartacking very near both ends.

8. From the right side, center the belt top over the right side of the lips and fuse in place using a press cloth. Top-stitch around the boxes on the outside of the buttonholes. Fuse the wrong side of the under belt to the back of the buttonholes.

9. With wrong sides together, serge around all sides of the belt with a narrow satin stitch to match the buttonhole lips.

10. Attach the buttons to match the buttonholes.

Lesson 34. Serged Elastic Button Loops

For a baby garment or a delicate feminine effect, serge-finish an edge with elastic thread in the lower looper. Then simply pull out elastic button loops at desired intervals for a quick and easy decorative closure.

1. Prepare your serger with decorative thread in the upper looper, elastic thread in the lower looper, and all-purpose or serger thread in the needle.

2. Adjust for a short, medium- to wide-width stitch. We prefer the 3-thread, although a 4-thread overedge stitch looks fine as well. Balance the tension with the upper looper thread slightly wrapping the edge. This makes the elastic invisible from the top side.

 Special Tip: You might have to play with the lower looper (elastic thread) tension to get it adjusted properly because the thread stretches so easily. Even then, the lower looper thread loops probably will not be precisely even due to the nature of elastic thread. If you cannot loosen the lower looper tension enough, take the elastic thread out of the tension control or a thread guide. Apply a little more tension by wrapping it entirely around a thread guide.

3. After testing the stitch, serge-finish one side of the closure.

4. Use pins to mark equidistant button placements along the outer edge of the serged elastic loops. With a fine crochet hook or tapestry needle, pull the elastic thread at each mark to form small, even loops. (Fig. 7-20) Pulling the elastic thread narrows and tightens the decorative edge slightly and anchors the loops.

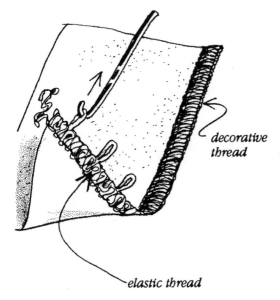

Fig. 7-20: Serge-finish one edge with elastic thread in the lower looper. Pull the elastic to form loops.

5. Change to all-purpose or serger thread in the lower looper and readjust the stitch to match the width and appearance of the decorative serging on the looped edge (now narrower than originally serged because you have pulled the loops).

6. Serge-finish the opposite closure edge. Sew small buttons in the middle of the row of stitching to match the elastic loop placements.

Project: Serge-finished Collar

Select a pretty place mat or dresser scarf for this simple collar. Use serged elastic button loops for the closure. Position the closure on either the front or back of the collar. (Fig. 7-21)

Fig. 7-21: This place-mat collar features a serged elastic button-loop closure.

Foot: Standard
Plate: Standard
Stitch: 3-thread
Stitch length: Short
Stitch width: Widest
Thread: Matching color
   Needle: All-purpose or serger
   Upper looper: Woolly nylon
   Lower looper: Elastic for looped closure; all-purpose or serger for serge-finishing
Tension: Balanced
Needle: Size 11/75

Fabric: One place mat or dresser scarf with crocheted edging, eyelet, Battenburg lace, or other decorative detailing

Notions: Five or more 7/16" ball buttons

1. Using a basic jewel-neckline pattern, cut the neckline and shoulder edges for the front and back collar. (Fig. 7-22) Trim 1/2" of the seam allowance from the neckline. Cut along the center front or back for the collar opening.

2. Serge-seam the shoulders with a medium-length, balanced stitch.

3. Adjust your serger for serged elastic button loops. Serge-finish the right front or the right back.

4. Pull the elastic thread at equidistant intervals to form button loops. The number of loops and their spacing depend on the depth of your collar and the desired effect.

5. Rethread the lower looper and readjust for matching decorative stitching. Serge-finish the other side of the opening.

6. Fold 1/8" of the neckline to the wrong side and serge-finish with the same stitch adjustment as in step 5. Thread the chain tails back through the stitches to secure.

7. Attach buttons to match the loop placements.

pattern back

pattern front

place mat

Fig. 7-22: *Cut the collar front and back from a place mat or dresser scarf.*

8. Expanding Your Artistic Possibilities

- **Lesson 35. Serger Chain Art**
- **Lesson 36. Serged Appliqué**
- **Lesson 37. Serger Cutwork**
- **Lesson 38. Embellished Fabric**

In previous chapters, we discussed traditional decorative seaming, edge-finishing, and special techniques. We also included a number of brand-new serger applications that we discovered during our research for this book series. Serge-bound seams and edges, clear elastic trim and piping, picot braid, and serged elastic button loops are some notable examples.

For this final chapter, we will cover creative possibilities that usually aren't associated with serger sewing. Although we had done some work with serger chain, appliqué, cutwork, and fabric embellishment in the past (see our two books, ***Distinctive Serger Gifts & Crafts*** and ***Simply Serge Any Fabric***), we felt that we had barely begun to explore these areas.

Having the time to test and develop more ideas was the major factor limiting our research. Yet artistic possibilities seem endless, including combinations of decorative techniques and unusual applications for existing techniques, as well as the continual introduction of new products and technology. What we have included in these last four lessons is merely a starting point—for us and, we hope, for you—to push the serger to its creative limits.

Lesson 35. Serger Chain Art

Originally used for professional-looking button and belt loops, serger chain art has now become an exciting medium for artistic expression in both craft and dressmaking projects. With the wide array of decorative threads and yarns available for serger use, possibilities abound for interesting chain projects. And the speedy serger can make yards and yards of serger chain in minimal time.

Now we've begun to explore serger-chain tassels, fringe, cording, and jewelry. (Fig. 8-1) Although

Fig. 8-1: *Artistic uses for serger chain include tassels, fringe, cording, and jewelry.*

some of these projects are more craft-oriented, others can be used to ornament your latest fashion garments. And you won't have to worry about not finding the perfect color or texture—you can coordinate it yourself.

1. To make a conventional serger thread chain, set your machine for a 3-thread rolled edge.

2. Put the thread, yarn, or ribbon you want to feature in the upper looper. This thread will be the most visible in the chain. Anything you can serge with is possible. Try ribbon floss, fine yarn, or any decorative thread.

3. Thread the needle with a lightweight matching or monofilament nylon thread. This thread will be the least visible in the chain. For variety,

test other lightweight threads. Fine metallic thread adds a touch of sparkle, while top-stitching thread changes the texture or color.

4. Use woolly or monofilament nylon in the lower looper for the tightest rolled-edge stitch and the firmest chain. Tighten the lower looper tension as much as possible when using shiny thread such as rayon in the upper looper.

 Special Tip: You may find it impossible to form a tightly rolled edge with a slippery thread in the upper looper. If so, try instead to make a flatter chain by tightening the upper looper tension, too, for a more balanced stitch.

5. Adjust your stitch length and tensions for the thread you're using. If you have difficulty starting because of your decorative thread, serge a few inches on fabric, then chain off. (Fig. 8-2) When using heavy thread such as

Fig. 8-2: *To begin, serge a few inches on fabric, then chain off.*

pearl cotton or crochet thread, start with a stitch length of 3mm and shorten it gradually to get the most attractive stitch formation. If the stitch length is too short, the thread can jam at the presser foot.

6. Hold the thread taut behind the presser foot for a more uniform chain. If there are skipped stitches in the chain, try switching to a size 14/90 needle. Also try loosening the tensions a small amount, one at a time. First adjust the lower looper, then the upper looper, and finally the needle.

Test unusual serger-chain stitching options. Vary the stitch size and tensions. Try serging over one or more strands of heavy filler thread. (Thread the filler thread through the presser foot.) Or, for more options, substitute fine wire for the filler thread. (We'll use fine wire later in this lesson to wrap a tassel.) Puffed serged braid (page 105) is actually a serger-chain variation made with balanced tension and a thicker filler.

Thread-chain cording

Make cording from serger thread chain by using the bobbin winder on your sewing machine.

1. Knot one or more long strands of serger chain through a hole in the bobbin. (Fig. 8-3) The strand(s) should be twice as long as the desired cording length. The length of the strand is limited by the length of your arms, unless you have one person run the machine while another holds the chain.

Fig. 8-3: Attach serged chain strands to the bobbin and wind. Hold the cording at the halfway point and wind the outer half back onto the bobbin half.

2. Hold the free end of the serger chain securely. Wind the bobbin until the strands are firmly twisted.

3. Before removing the cording from the bobbin, hold the twisted strands at the halfway point with your other hand. The cording will automatically twist back on itself. Pull the cording until the twisting is uniform.

Thread-chain cording may be used for decorative accents (such as edge trimming or couching), accessory items (necklaces or belts), or home decoration (pillow trims and drapery tie-backs).

Special Tip: For heavy cording that is too thick to tie to a bobbin, have one person hold one end of the strand(s) while another person does the twisting. Or tie one end to a doorknob on a closed door and twist from the free end.

Thread-chain fringe

Make your own matching or decorative fringe from serger thread chain. For 1" fringe, cut a piece of tear-away stabilizer 3" wide by the desired length. Fold it lengthwise into a 1" width (3 layers). Vary the width of the stabilizer to change the length of the fringe. Wrap the serger chain around the stabilizer. With a medium- to wide-width satin, balanced stitch, serge along one edge with the same decorative thread in the upper looper. (Fig. 8-4) Dab seam sealant on the

chains on the other edge so they won't unravel. Allow them to dry, then cut. Tear away the stabilizer. Top-stitch the fringe to your project through the upper row of stitching.

Thread-chain tassels

Make tassels from any size serger thread chain. (Fig. 8-5) For a delicate tassel, use rayon, lingerie, or fine metallic thread. Try pearl cotton, pearl rayon, or crochet thread for a heavier tassel. Rayon thread will make the smoothest chain. Serge at least six yards of chain for one tassel. Smaller chain will require more strands for a fuller appearance.

tear-away stabilizer layers

serge

cut

tear stabilizer

Fig. 8-4: *Wrap the chain around the stabilizer. Serge the upper edge and cut the lower edge. Tear away the stabilizer for the finished fringe.*

Fig. 8-5: *Make tassels from any size serger chain.*

1. Loosely wind the chain over a firm piece of cardboard cut to the length of your tassel. The more chain that is wrapped, the fuller the tassel. Do not stretch the chain while winding.

2. Cut a 6" strand of chain for the tassel hanger. Tie the chain together at end of the cardboard, or tie a knot, leaving a loop for a hanger, as shown. (Fig. 8-6) Dab seam sealant on the

Fig. 8-6: Tie the chain together at one end of the cardboard.

chains on the opposite end of the cardboard so they won't unravel. Allow them to dry before cutting.

3. About 3/4" below the tied ends, form a loop of chain and wrap over it. After you have completed the wrapping, thread the chain ends through the loop and pull to secure. (Fig. 8-7) Hide the ends under the edge of the wrapping.

 Optional: Serge an 8" chain strand over fine wire. Wrap the tassel, twist the ends together, and tuck them under the wrapping.

Fig. 8-7: Form a thread-chain loop and wrap over it. Pull the ends through the loop to secure. Tuck the tails under the wrapping.

Project: Double-wrapped Tassel

Make two tassels to finish the ends of the table runner in Lesson 17, page 91. (Fig. 8-8) Test matching metallic

Fig. 8-8: These simple thread chain tassels feature two wrappings. Attach them to the table runner from Lesson 17.

yarn in a chain before using it for the tassels. If you find that it is too wiry, opt for a matching color of softer heavy rayon thread.

Foot: Standard
Plate: Rolled edge
Stitch: 3-thread
Stitch length: Short (1 - 2mm)
Stitch width: Narrow (1.8mm or 2mm)
Thread: Matching color
  Needle: All-purpose or serger
  Upper looper: Decorative thread
  Lower looper: Woolly nylon
Tension: Rolled edge
Needle: Size 11/75
Notions: 16" of 24-gauge fine, flexible wire (such as bead wire, purchased at a craft store); a small amount of yarn in a matching color (enough to form two 3/4" balls); cardboard

1. Serge 22 yards of chain for two tassels. With the same serger adjustments and decorative thread, carefully serge over the wire.

2. Cut off 48" of chain and section it into four 12" pieces.

3. For each tassel, loosely wrap half the long chain around a 5" piece of cardboard. Tie the chains together at one side of the cardboard using one of the shorter chains. See Fig. 8-6.

4. Dab seam sealant on the thread chains at the opposite end so they won't unravel. Allow them to dry, then cut the ends evenly.

5. With the other 12" chains, wrap each tassel together tightly about 3/4" from the top. Secure the ends by

placing them through the loop, as shown in step 3 of the thread-chain tassel instructions on page 154.

6. Wind the matching yarn into balls and insert them between the thread-chain strands close to the wrapped sections.

7. With 8" of the wire, wrap each tassel tightly, enclosing and securing the yarn ball. Insert the wire ends under the wrapped edges. Adjust the thread chains to cover the yarn. (Fig. 8-9) (Or use two additional 12" chains to wrap the tassels as in step 5 above.)

Twist wire ends together and tuck under

Fig. 8-9: *Use chain serged over fine wire to wrap tassels.*

8. Hand-tack the tassels to each end of the table runner, covering the serging joints.

Lesson 36.
Serged Appliqué

Appliqué is one of our favorite embellishments because it offers so many options for creativity. You can use it to add texture, color, and a three-dimensional effect to any fabric. Fashion your own design to adorn your latest garments, sweaters, accessories, or home decoration projects.

In the past, we've worked with flat and 3-D appliqué. We've also tried padded appliqué. Just about any serged edge-finish or trim can be used. Other techniques such as serger lace and serging over sequins, beads, or pearls adapt well to appliqué. Let your creativity guide you.

Serge-finish the edges of the pieces you plan to appliqué. A satin rolled-edge stitch is the most common for edge finishing, but any serged edge is possible.

Apply the appliqué pieces to your fabric by top-stitching all of the edges flat, top-stitching only part of the edges (for a raised or 3-D appliqué), or attaching them by hand-tacking, fusing, or fabric painting. (Fig. 8-10)

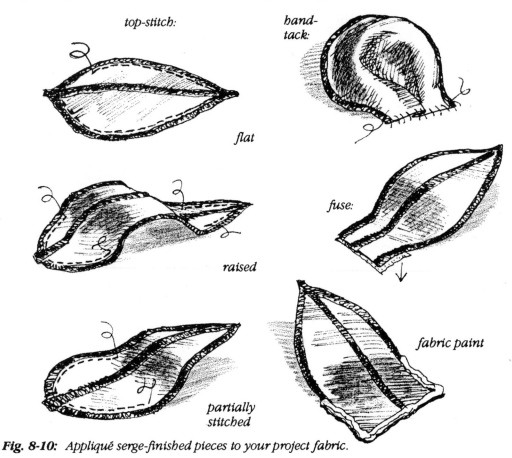

top-stitch:

flat

hand-tack:

raised

fuse:

partially stitched

fabric paint

Fig. 8-10: *Appliqué serge-finished pieces to your project fabric.*

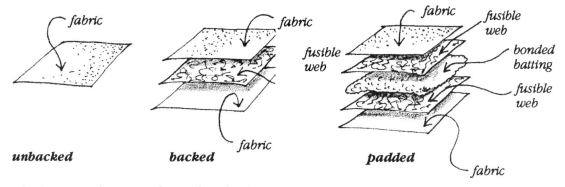

fabric

fabric

fabric

fusible web

fusible web

bonded batting

fusible web

fusible web

fabric

fabric

unbacked   **backed**   **padded**

Fig. 8-11: Appliqués can be cut from backed, unbacked, or padded fabric.

Appliqués may be unbacked, backed, or padded. (Fig. 8-11) Unbacked appliqués are usually applied flat to the project fabric with the under side of the appliqué fabric hidden. Make backed appliqués simply by sandwiching a layer of fusible transfer web between two layers of fabric (right sides out) so that both sides of the appliqué will appear finished when they are applied by the raised or 3-D methods.

Make padded appliqués by sandwiching bonded batting between two layers of fusible transfer web. Then fuse the batting and web between two layers of fabric, with the web against the wrong side of the fabric. Padded appliqués are most often applied raised or 3-D, in the same manner as unpadded, backed appliqués.

Project: Appliquéd Evening Bag

Serged appliqué adorns this unique evening bag. Make the strap by cording thread chain, then top the bag with the pearl-trimmed organdy flower made in Lesson 28 (page 130). (Fig. 8-12)

Fig. 8-12: Construct an appliquéd evening bag with a cording strap, satin leaves, and the flower from Lesson 28.

Foot: Rolled edge for appliqué; standard for serge-seaming

Plate: Rolled edge for appliqué; standard for serge-seaming

Stitch: 3-thread for appliqué; 3- or 4-thread for serge-seaming

Stitch length: Short (1 - 2mm) for appliqué; medium (2.5 - 3mm) for serge-seaming

Stitch width: Narrow (1.8mm or 2mm) for appliqué; wide (4mm or 5mm) for serge-seaming

Thread: Matching color
  Needle(s): All-purpose or serger
  Upper looper: Rayon or other decorative for appliqué; all-purpose or serger for serge-seaming
  Lower looper: Woolly nylon for appliqué; all-purpose or serger for serge-seaming

Tension: Rolled edge for appliqué; balanced for serge-seaming

Needle(s): Size 11/75

Fabric: 1/2 yard taffeta for outer bag; 1/2 yard matching lining fabric for bag lining; 1/6 yard matching satin for appliquéd leaves

Notions: 10" polyester fleece; 10" heavy fusible interfacing; 6" by 12" piece paper-backed fusible web; one spool matching ribbon floss for strap; one large snap

1. Cut 10" by 18" rectangles from the taffeta, lining, fleece, and interfacing. Fuse the interfacing to the fleece.

2. From the ribbon floss, make one yard of thread-chain cording, following the instructions on page 152.

3. Match the ends of the cording to the cut edges of the right side of the lining 6-1/2" from the top on both sides. (Fig. 8-13) With the right sides of the taffeta and lining together, place the fleece on top of the taffeta.

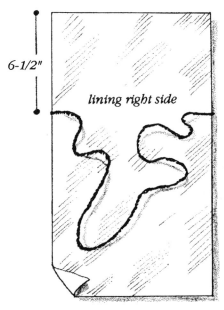

6-1/2"

lining right side

Fig. 8-13: *Position the cording on top of the lining.*

4. Serge-seam the four sides of the bag, leaving an opening at the lower edge for turning and being careful not to catch the cording in the serging. Secure the cording in the seam by straight-stitching again over the cording with a short stitch length.

5. Turn the bag to the right side and fold the opening allowances to the inside. Press carefully. Edge-stitch across the lower edge, closing the opening.

6. At the lower edge, fold 4-1/2" to the wrong side to form the bag. From the right side of the bag, edge-stitch the three unfolded edges. (Fig. 8-14)

Fig. 8-14: Fold up the lower edge to form a pocket. Edge-stitch.

7. Fold the upper edge down even with the cording placement, forming the flap. Press lightly.

8. To make the leaf appliqué, fuse the transfer web to the back of the satin fabric. Remove the paper backing and fuse the other side to the wrong side of a matching rectangle of the satin. Using the grid as a pattern, cut one large leaf and one small leaf set from the fused satin. (Fig. 8-15)

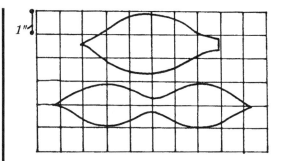

Fig. 8-15: Pattern for the large leaf and small leaf set.

9. With your serger adjusted for appliqué sewing (see specifications on page 158), fold the leaves in half lengthwise and serge the folded edge, forming the leaf ribs. (Fig. 8-16) Pull the leaves flat and serge-finish all leaf edges.

Fig. 8-16: Fold the leaf in half and serge the fold with a satin rolled edge.

10. Place the large leaf on the bag flap, raising the center rib three-dimensionally. Top-stitch both sides, starting and ending about 1-1/2" from the leaf ends.

11. Pin a tuck in the middle of the smaller leaf set and place it over the larger leaf, as shown. (Fig. 8-17) Top-stitch both leaves as you did the larger one. Straight-stitch across the bottom of all three leaves to secure.

Fig. 8-17: Appliqué the leaves to the bag flap.

12. Attach the flower made in Lesson 28 over the center of the leaves. Hand-sew the large snap, securing the flap to the top of the bag.

Lesson 37.
Serger Cutwork

Our first introduction to serger cutwork was when Sue Green wrote about it for our *Serger Update* newsletter in early 1988. Although it was a

fascinating technique, it took considerable skill and patience to serge-finish the inner edge of small holes cut in a piece of fabric. (Fig. 8-18)

Then we discovered an interesting new product—water-soluble stabilizer—and Naomi started experimenting. The results were a speedy combination of sewing and serging that created an interesting new appliquéd cutwork. (Fig. 8-18)

difficult serge-finishing method

easy water-soluble stabilizer method

Fig. 8-18: Serger cutwork options.

This newer method works equally well for garments, table linens, and craft projects. The cutwork appliqué must be applied to a washable fabric, because the washable stabilizer has to be dissolved in water to complete the project.

Serging over the stabilizer gives stitches a stiff, starched effect. Test various threads and stitch types for the desired effect. For example, woolly nylon in a satin rolled edge creates a stiff design. With a longer, balanced stitch, it gives a softer appearance.

1. With a water-soluble pen, draw a cutwork design outline on the project fabric. (Fig. 8-19)

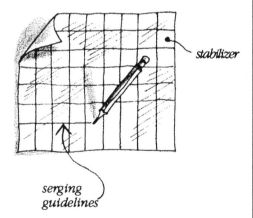

Fig. 8-19: Draw cutwork outlines on the fabric and serging guidelines on the water-soluble stabilizer.

2. Cut a piece of water-soluble stabilizer at least 1" larger than the design on all sides.

3. Draw serging guidelines onto the stabilizer. (Fig. 8-19) For more durability, draw the guidelines close together and limit the size of the appliqué. Plan straight rows of serging for your first project because serging a curved fold can by tricky.

4. Fold the stabilizer on the guidelines and serge over the folds with a stitch adjustment you have previously tested. (Don't worry if you cut the stabilizer.)

5. Pull the stabilizer flat, stretching it over the outline on the right side of the base fabric. Pin it in place. (Fig. 8-20) Be sure the serged stitches extend past the design outline on all sides.

Fig. 8-20: Pin the serged stabilizer over the cutwork outline. Zigzag it to the fabric.

6. With matching thread and a narrow, satin stitch, zigzag the stabilizer to the fabric following the design outline.

7. Trim the stabilizer close to the outside of the zigzag stitch. Be careful not to cut the zigzag stitch or the fabric. (Fig. 8-21)

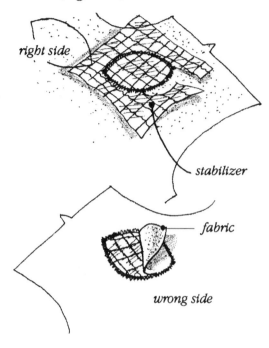

Fig. 8-21: Trim the stabilizer outside the zigzagging on the front. Trim the fabric inside the zigzagging on the back.

8. Carefully trim away the fabric from behind the stabilizer appliqué. To finish and secure the cutwork, stitch over the original zigzagging from the right side. Use a narrow, satin zigzag stitch just a little wider than the original stitching in step 6.

9. Submerge the cutwork appliqué in water to remove the stabilizer. Allow it to air dry, or press it dry between two layers of press cloth.

Project: Cutwork Tablecloth

Feature a cutwork motif on one or more corners of a square card-table cloth. Or change measurements for an elegant dresser scarf. (Fig. 8-22)

Fig. 8-22: Embellish a tablecloth with appliquéd cutwork.

Foot: Rolled edge
Plate: Rolled edge
Stitch: 3-thread rolled edge
Stitch length: Short (1 - 2mm)
Stitch width: Narrow (1.8mm or 2mm)
Thread: Matching color
   Needle: All-purpose or serger
   Upper looper: All-purpose or serger
   Lower looper: All-purpose or serger
Tension: Rolled edge
Needle: Size 11/75
Fabric: 54" by 54" square light-weight linen-like fabric

Optional: Use a 14" by 54" rectangle of the same fabric for a dresser scarf.

Notions: One 6" by 6" square water-soluble stabilizer; air-erasable or water-soluble marker

1. Serge-finish all four edges of the fabric with a narrow rolled edge, serging on and off at each corner. Secure the thread chains with seam sealant and clip the tails when dry.

2. Draw a 4" oval in the corner of the tablecloth using the marker.

3. Serge the stabilizer with rows of stitching in a crisscrossed design of your choice. Extend the rows of serging to fill the stabilizer square.

4. Center the serged stabilizer over the oval. Stretch it and pin the edges. Zigzag around the oval with a short, narrow stitch.

5. Carefully cut away the serged stabilizer outside the oval, next to the zigzag stitching. On the back, trim the fabric from underneath the stabilizer inside the oval.

6. With a slightly wider satin-length zigzag, stitch over the original zigzagging.

7. Soak the design in water to remove the stabilizer. Let dry, or carefully press between two press cloths.

Lesson 38. Embellished Fabric

Although there is a difference between actually constructing yardage on your serger and ornamenting fabric by adding serged stitches and detail, we group them together here.

Constructing fabric

Using a serger to construct patchwork fabric has been explored in detail by many sewing professionals. Myriad patchwork designs are possible, and they can be constructed more quickly than with a sewing machine because of the serger's faster stitching.

Another option for constructing decorative fabric on your serger is to mix fabric types, textures, or colors to complement the design of your garment. The method of seaming the elements together can be decorative as well. Exposed seams of any type or color are an option.

Inserts are yet another way to create unusual fabric for your project. Strips of synthetic suede or leather can be placed strategically in the middle of your fashion fabric. Tapestry insets add a hand-detailed effect. Or a lighter-weight fabric strip can be serge-gathered on both long edges and inserted as a decorative detail. (Fig. 8-23)

Fig. 8-23: *Serge-gather a fabric strip and inset into yardage.*

Ornamenting fabric

Heirloom serging (a replication of French hand-sewing) was an early example of serger-embellished fabric. Delicate rows of pintucks, lace inserts, and rolled edges are quickly applied to a fabric such as batiste, organdy, or handkerchief linen. An art in itself, beautiful heirloom serging has been featured extensively in books and articles.

We want to take the art of ornamenting fabric one step further. You don't have to use dainty stitches on lightweight woven fabrics in straight rows in order to embellish your fabric. Consider all of your ornamental serging possibilities. Most edge-finishes also can be serged over folds, so you have the option of placing stitches anywhere on your fabric— and in any direction.

Try diagonal or vertical rows of corded rolled edges, perhaps to accent a stripe in the fabric. Test parallel rows of wide, balanced, satin serging to duplicate current designer fabrics. (Or try prepleating a fabric

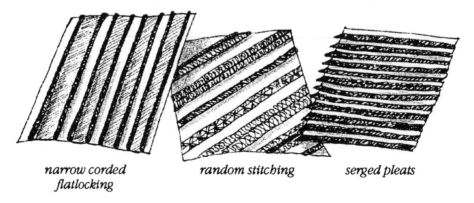

narrow corded flatlocking   random stitching   serged pleats

Fig. 8-24: *Ornament fabrics with corded flatlocking on stripes, random diagonal stitches, or narrow serged pleats.*

with a *Perfect Pleater* device and serge-finishing each tuck.) Consider serging with uneven spacing, sporadically placed stitching, or combinations of techniques. (Fig. 8-24, page 164)

Experiment with all fabric types and any decorative thread. Test ideas from ready-to-wear. Let your imagination soar. We include a few test results here, but these are only the beginning. There's plenty of room for innovation in serger sewing. Have fun, experiment, and let us know what you discover.

Chain-loop serging—Our first idea for this technique was to serge on and off a fold or edge, using a satin rolled edge and leaving thread-chain loops at intervals along the stitching. We serged for a distance and then chained off the fabric. To form a loop, we raised the presser foot, anchored the needle right where the chain left the fabric, and began serging again.

Although we achieved an interesting effect (Fig. 8-25), the method was slow and tedious. Naomi discovered a faster, more random effect by raising

Fig. 8-25: Serge on and off your fabric for a chain-loop detail.

the front of the presser foot only to insert the fabric. She was also successful serging with the presser foot off the entire time. She was able to chain off and on easily. Leave the chain in loops or cut it at varying lengths. Don't worry if you cut the fabric while serging; the rolled edge covers any cuts. We've used this technique for the scarf project that follows.

Flatlocked patches—With a heavier thread such as pearl rayon in the upper looper, create short patches of flatlocking in the middle of your fabric, leaving thread tails at each end. Tie beads onto the tails for an added ornamental touch. (Fig. 8-26) Mark

Fig. 8-26: Flatlock random patches on your fabric. Tie beads onto the tails.

the placement of your flatlocked patches or apply them randomly. Fold along the placement line. Remove the stitches from the stitch finger manually or by pressing the tension-release lever and pull out about 3" of unchained thread. Raise the presser foot and anchor the needle at the end of the placement line.

Flatlock the patch, lift the presser foot, remove the stitches from the stitch finger, and pull the threads away from the serging. Do not chain off. Knot the threads at each end or attach beads to secure the stitching.

Try decorative patches using a rolled-edge or narrow, balanced stitch. Or try chaining on and off the fabric for a different effect.

Finger tensioning—We used finger tensioning to gather lightweight fabric in Lesson 23 (page 111). It also can be used to vary the look of your decorative stitching.

First we tried applying tension on the looper threads, but had little success. We then went back to the needle thread (used for tension gathering) and pressed the thread against the face of the machine just above the needle bar. By putting tension on the needle thread of a narrow flatlock at equal intervals, we achieved a scalloped flatlocked effect. (Fig. 8-27)

Fig. 8-27: *Use finger tensioning for a scalloped flatlock.*

Don't be afraid to try other methods for varying your decorative stitch at intervals during your serging. Try using both a rolled edge and a bal-anced stitch. Test with different threads, stitch widths, and lengths.

Charted needlework variation—Those serger enthusiasts who have done charted needlework on the sewing machine may want to explore its application for the serger.

As long as the needle fits between the edge of the bed and the serger needle (and the looper can pass over it), you can serge charted needlework. The largest size needle you will be able to use depends upon your model. We found a variance from a #8 on the 734D to a #5 on the 534.

To make loops on a fold of fabric, remove the presser foot. Your stitch adjustment should be similar to a reversible-edge binding stitch (page 69). Hold a knitting needle along the edge of the cutter to the right of the serger needle. Butt a fold of fabric up against the left side of the knitting needle. Serge slowly, catching the fold with the serged stitching. (Fig. 8-28)

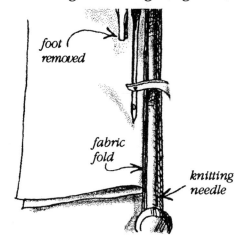

Fig. 8-28: *Serge over a knitting needle, catching the looped stitches in the fold of the fabric.*

Note: Test by hand first to be certain the stitch is adjusted correctly and that the needle and looper clear the knitting needle.

Without removing the knitting needle from the stitching, fold again near the first row and repeat the instructions above using a second needle. (Because the knitting needle can be held securely against the edge of the bed, serging over charted needles can be easier for a beginner than sewing over them.)

By serging over two needles with woolly nylon in the loopers, we easily created an interesting raised trim. (Fig. 8-29)

Fig. 8-29: Create an interesting raised trim by serging over knitting needles with woolly nylon.

We know there are many more possibilities for serging raised stitches over needles, so put your imagination to work.

Project: Embellished Chiffon Scarf

Embellish a fashionable two-yard chiffon scarf with random decorative serging for an attention-getting accessory. (Fig. 8-30)

Fig. 8-30: Add free-form embellishment to a long chiffon scarf.

Foot: Rolled edge
Plate: Rolled edge
Stitch: 3-thread
Stitch length: Short (1 - 2mm)
Stitch width: Narrow
Thread: Contrasting color
   Needle: All-purpose or serger
   Upper looper: Woolly nylon
   Lower looper: Woolly nylon
Tension: Rolled edge
Needle: Size 11/75
Fabric: 2 yards chiffon
Notions: Optional—ornamental
   beads to tie on thread-chain tails

1. Cut a piece of chiffon the length of the fabric by 18" wide. Finish all four sides with a rolled edge.

2. Using the techniques described above under chain-loop serging, fill the scarf with random rows of decorative serging. The serging need not be done on the straight of grain. Let a random pattern add to the decorative effect.

3. Leave the chain loops or clip them apart at varying lengths. Tie on ornamental beads if desired.

White Superlock *History*

Thomas H. White, a visionary leader in the sewing machine industry, founded White Sewing in 1858. In 1866 he moved the company to Cleveland, Ohio, and incorporated as White Sewing Machine Company in 1876.

The name of the parent company was changed to White Consolidated Industries in 1964, reflecting the eminent growth that would acquire such well-known companies as Kelvinator, Gibson, and others, making WCI a billion-dollar corporation.

In 1986 White Sewing Machine Company merged with Husqvarna (Viking) Sewing Machine Company to form the current parent company, VWS, Inc. Both companies had already contributed more than 100 years of experience, innovation, and quality to the home-sewing industry.

Along with its many other innovations, in the 1980s White pioneered an overlock machine specially designed for the home-sewing market. The *Superlock* Model 534 cut sewing time in half—seaming, trimming, and overcasting in one easy operation. This popular model was the first serger to offer a 3/4-thread capability, numbered tension dials, and a recessed cutting system.

The *White Superlock* set a precedent in serger sewing by providing optional time-saving accessories, including the blindhem, elastic, piping, and pearl/sequin feet. Today, a new generation of innovative *White Superlocks* features highly visible threading, swing-away cutting blades, and a tension-release lever.

Glossary of Serging Terms

All-purpose or serger thread—All-purpose thread usually means cotton-covered polyester wound parallel on conventional spools. Standard serger thread has the same fiber content but is lighter in weight than all-purpose thread and is cross-wound on cones or tubes so that it can feed more easily during higher-speed serger sewing.

Balanced stitch—A serge-finished edge or seam in which the upper- and lower-looper thread tensions are balanced so the threads meet at the edge of the fabric, forming loops.

Binding—A strip of fabric sewn to an edge, then wrapped around it and secured to hide the seam and the raw edge.

Bite—The distance between the cutter and the needle, affecting the amount of fabric in the stitch.

Decorative seam (also decorative exposed seam)—Any seam on the outside of a garment or project that enhances design detail.

Decorative thread (also decorative serging or decorative finish)—Any thread other than all-purpose or serger thread, although even a contrasting color of these threads is technically considered decorative. Our favorite decorative threads include woolly nylon, rayon, pearl cotton, silk, buttonhole twist, and metallic. New threads are introduced regularly.

Edge-stitch—A medium-length (10-12 stitches/inch) straight stitch on a conventional sewing machine applied near the edge of anything being sewn. Edge-stitching is often used to join two serge-finished layers.

Filler-cord—Crochet thread, pearl cotton, or buttonhole twist that simulates piping when serged over with a short (satin) stitch.

Flatlock—A technique by which the needle thread is loose enough to flatten out on top of the fabric, forming decorative loops, when the fabric is pulled apart. The underside will show a ladder effect of evenly spaced double parallel stitches. Used for both seaming and decorative stitching on a folded edge, flatlocking lends many creative possibilities. A 3-thread (and even 4-thread) stitch can be adjusted to flatlock.

Heavy thread—Crochet thread, pearl cotton, or buttonhole twist used for serge-gathering or filler-cord in serger piping.

Long stitch—A 4-5mm serged stitch length.

Machine baste—A long (6-8 stitches/inch) straight stitch on a conventional sewing machine.

Mail order—A growing trend that offers the convenience of at-home catalog shopping. Almost any product is available through mail order, but without the immediate, hands-on selection available at your local fabric store.

Matching thread—Thread the same color as (or that blends as well as possible with) the project fabric.

Medium-length stitch—A 2.5-3mm serged stitch length.

Medium-width stitch—A 2.8mm or 3.5mm serged stitch width.

Narrow-width stitch—A 1.8mm or 2mm serged stitch width. Used to serge a narrow seam or edge.

Ornamental serging (also decorative serging)—Any serger stitching used to artistically enhance a garment or project. Decorative thread, altered tension, or a combination of serging techniques can be used to create ornamental serging.

Ready-to-wear—Garments available for purchase through retail stores and mail-order outlets.

Rolled edge (finish or seam)—Also called a narrow rolled edge or hem, this stitch is created by altering the tension so that the raw edge rolls to the underside. A short stitch length creates an attractive satin-stitch edge.

Satin stitch (satin length)—A stitch length short enough to allow the thread used to cover the entire fabric over which it is serged. Appropriate for both a balanced stitch or a rolled edge.

Serge-finish—Most often a medium-length, medium-width, and balanced 3- or 4-thread stitch used to finish the edge of one layer during the construction process.

Serge-gather—Several serger techniques are possible for gathering an edge. If your serger has a differential feed, use the 2.0 setting. Another option is to tighten your needle tension and lengthen your stitch. Or simply serge over heavy thread with a balanced stitch, being careful not to catch the heavy thread in the serging. Then, after anchoring one end, pull the heavy thread to gather the edge to any specific length. A fourth option is to loosen the needle tension, serge, and then pull up the needle thread.

Serge-seam—As in serge-finish, a medium-length, medium-width, and balanced 3- or 4-thread stitch, but in this case it's used to seam two layers together.

Short stitch—A 1-2mm serged stitch length.

Stitch-in-the-ditch—Stitching directly on top of a previous seam to secure another layer positioned on the underside. Often used for nearly invisible stitching when applying a binding to an edge.

Straight stitch—A medium-length (10-12 stitches/inch) straight stitch on a conventional sewing machine.

Thread chain—The joined loops formed by serging on a properly threaded machine with no fabric.

Top-stitch—A conventional-machine straight stitch (10-12 stitches/inch) used to attach one layer (often serge-finished) to another. Top-stitching also can be used as a decorative design detail.

Wide stitch—A 4mm or 5mm serged stitch width.

Woolly nylon—One of our favorite decorative threads that became popular with the advent of serger sewing. A crimped nylon thread, it fluffs out to fill in any see-through spaces on a decorative edge.

Zigzag stitch—A basic stitch on a conventional sewing machine that forms a back-and-forth pattern similar to herringbone.

Mail-Order Resources

We recommend that every serger enthusiast develop a special relationship with his or her local dealers and retailers for convenient advice and inspiration, plus the ease of coordinating purchases. However, when specialty items cannot be found locally, or when a home-sewer lives several miles from a sewing retailer, mail-order specialists are a worthwhile option.

The following list will make your search for these resources a breeze. Our list is for reference only and does not carry our endorsement or guarantee. (We have not knowingly included any questionable items or firms.)

 Special Tip: To streamline information gathering, be specific even when simply requesting samples or specific product brochures. Let the company know exactly what you are looking for, such as color, fiber, texture, or size.

Risk-free Mail Order

■ **Before you buy:** Read catalog descriptions carefully to make sure the product is what you want. Is there a guarantee? What is the policy for returns?

■ **Placing your order:** Fill out the order form carefully and make a copy of both order and payment for future reference. Never send cash. When ordering by phone, complete the order form first to prevent mistakes. If possible, keep a record of the date of your phone order, as well as the name of the salesperson.

■ **If there is a problem with your order:** Contact the company right away, by phone or by mail. If you contact by phone, be sure to record the time and date of your call, as well as the name of the contact person. Follow up in writing, describing the problem and outlining any solution reached during the phone call. Send copies of your order and payment record. Get a return receipt from the shipper when returning merchandise.

■ **The "30-Day Rule":** If a delivery date isn't given in a company's materials, the company must ship within 30 days of receiving your order (COD orders excepted), according to the Federal Trade Commission's Mail Order Merchandise Rule. If you place an order using a credit card, your account shouldn't be billed until shipment is made. If you send payment with your order and your order doesn't arrive when promised, you may cancel the order and get a full refund.

 Authors' note: In today's volatile business climate, any mail-order source list will change frequently. Please send your comments on any out-of-business notifications or unsatisfactory service to Update Newsletters, 2269 Chestnut #269, San Francisco, CA 94123.

Key to Abbreviations and Symbols:

SASE= self-addressed, stamped (first-class) envelope

L-SASE = large SASE (2-oz. first-class postage)

* = refundable with order

= for information, brochure or catalog

 Note: Check with your postmaster regarding Canadian mail.

Serger Company

White Sewing Machine Company, Inc. (*White Superlock*)
11750 Berea Road
Cleveland, OH 44111

Great Serger Notions

Aardvark Adventures, P.O. Box 2449, Livermore, CA 94551, 415/443-2687. Books, beads, buttons, bangles, plus an unusual assortment of related products. Decorative serging thread, including metallics. $1#.

The Bee Lee Company, P.O. Box 36108-B, Dallas, TX 75235. Complete selection of threads, zippers, notions, and trims, including Western styles. Free#.

Bobette Industries, 2401 S. Hill St., Los Angeles, CA 90007-2785, toll-free in CA, 800/237-6462 (orders only). Notions, tools, threads, books, machine parts, and accessories. $1#.

Catherine's, Rt. 6, Box 1227, Lexington, NC 27292, 704/798-1595. Serger threads and more at wholesale prices. Minimum order $35. School quantity discounts. $2 and L-SASE for thread color card.

Clotilde, Inc., 1909 SW First Ave., Ft. Lauderdale, FL 33315, 305/761-8655. Catalog of over 1,200 items, including the *Perfect Pleater*, special serger threads and notions, sewing tools and supplies, and books and videos. $1#.

Custom Zips, P.O. Box 1200, So. Norwalk, CT 06856. Zippers cut to order. $2#.

The Cutting Edge, P.O. Box 76044, St. Peters, MO 63376. Serger notions, including coned threads (all-purpose and decorative), needle threaders, patterns, and carrying cases. L-SASE#.

D & E Distributing, 199 N. El Camino Real #F-242, Encinitas, CA 92024. Decorative threads and yarns, including silk, rayon, and Madeira metallics. L-SASE#.

The Embroidery Stop, 1042 Victory Dr., Yardley, PA 19067. Threads, yarns, and needles. $1#.

Fit For You, 781 Golden Prados Dr., Diamond Bar, CA 91795, 714/861-5021. Sewing notions, serger accessories, videos, and square-dance patterns. L-SASE#.

Home-Sew, Dept. S, Bethlehem, PA 18018. Basic notions, trims, coned serger threads, and tools. Free#.

Jacquart's, 505 E. McLeod, Ironwood, MI 49938, 906/932-1339. Zippers. $1#.

Maryland Trims, P.O. Box 3508, Silver Spring, MD 20901. Laces, sewing notions, and supplies. $1.75#.

Mill End Store, Box 02098, Portland, OR 97202, 503/236-1234. Broad selection of notions, trims, serger threads, and accessories. SASE#.

Nancy's Notions, Ltd., P.O. Box 683, Beaver Dam, WI 53916, 800/765-0690. Over 300 sewing notions and accessories, serger threads and tools, interfacings and fabrics, and books and videos. Free#.

National Thread & Supply, 695 Red Oak Rd., Stockbridge, GA 30281, 800/847-1001, ext. 1688; in GA, 404/389-9115. Name-brand sewing supplies and notions. Free#.

Newark Dressmaker Supply, P.O. Box 2448, Lehigh Valley, PA 18001, 215/837-7500. Sewing notions, trims, buttons, decorative threads, and serger supplies. Free#.

The Perfect Notion, 566 Hoyt St., Darien, CT 06820, 203/968-1257. Hard-to-find notions and serger threads (including its *ThreadFuse* fusible thread). $1#.

Serge and Sew Notions, 11285 96th Ave. N., Maple Grove, MN 55369, 800/969-7396. Serger threads, books, patterns, furniture, fabrics, and more, priced 20-40% below retail. $2.50*#. Swatch club, $6 for six months.

Serging Ahead, P.O. Box 45, Grandview, MO 64030. Serger threads, books, and patterns. $1#.

Sew-Art International, P.O. Box 550, Bountiful, UT 84010. Decorative threads, notions, and accessories. Free#.

Sew Craft, P.O. Box 1869, Warsaw, IN 46580, 219/269-4046. Books, decorative threads, and notions.

Sew-Fit Co., P.O. Box 565, La Grange, IL 60525, 312/579-3222. Sewing notions and accessories; modular tables for serger/sewing machine setup; books. Free#.

Sewing Emporium, 1087 Third Ave., Chula Vista, CA 92010, 619/420-3490. Hard-to-find sewing notions, sewing machine and serger cabinets and accessories, and serger threads and accessories. $2#.

The Sewing Place, 18870 Cox Ave., Saratoga, CA 95070. Sewing machine and serger needles and feet, plus books by Gale Grigg Hazen. Specify your brand and model if ordering machine accessories. L-SASE#.

The Sewing Workshop, 2010 Balboa St., San Francisco, CA 94121, 415/221-SEWS. Unique designer notions. L-SASE#.

Solo Slide Fasteners, Inc., P.O. Box 528, Stoughton, MA 02072, 800/343-9670. All types and lengths of zippers; other selected notions. Free#.

Speed Stitch, 3113-D Broadpoint Dr., Harbor Heights, FL 33983, 800/ 874-4115. Machine-art kits and supplies, including all-purpose, decorative, and specialty serging threads, books, and accessories. $3*#.

Thread Discount & Sales, 7105 S. Eastern, Bell Gardens, CA 90201, 213/562-3438. Coned polyester thread. SASE#.

Threads & Things, P.O. Box 83190, San Diego, CA 92138, 619/440-8760. 100% rayon thread. Free#.

Threads West, 422 E. State St., Redlands, CA 92373, 714/793-4405 or 0214. Coned thread, serger parts, and accessories. SASE for free thread color list.

Treadleart, 25834 Narbonne Ave., Suite I, Lomita, CA 90717, 800/327-4222. Books, serging supplies, notions, decorative threads, and creative inspiration. $1.50#.

T-Rific Products Co., P.O. Box 911, Winchester, OR 97495. Coned serger thread. Thread color chart, $1.25.

Two Brothers, 1602 Locust St., St. Louis, MO 63103. Zipper assortment. SASE#.

YLI Corporation, 482 North Freedom, Provo, UT 84601, 800/854-1932 or 801/377-3900. Decorative, specialty, serger, and all-purpose threads, yarns, and ribbons. $1.50#.

Other Publications by the Authors

Serger Update Newsletter, 2269 Chestnut #269, San Francisco, CA 94123. The only periodical devoted entirely to serging news and techniques. Published monthly ($39 annual subscription).

Sewing Update Newsletter (see address above). Newsletter format with tips and ideas from sewing professionals (sister publication to *Serger Update Newsletter*). Sent every other month —$19.50 per year.

Distinctive Serger Gifts & Crafts, Chilton Book Company, 1989. The first book with one-of-a-kind serger projects using ingenious methods and upscale ideas, by Naomi Baker and Tammy Young.

Innovative Serging, Chilton Book Company, 1989. State-of-the-art techniques for overlock sewing, by Gail Brown and Tammy Young.

Innovative Sewing, Chilton Book Company, 1990. The newest, best, and fastest sewing techniques, by Gail Brown and Tammy Young.

Know Your Baby Lock, Chilton Book Company, 1990. Ornamental serging techniques for all *baby lock* serger models, by Naomi Baker and Tammy Young.

Simply Serge Any Fabric, Chilton Book Company, 1990. Tips and techniques for successfully serging all types of fabric, by Naomi Baker and Tammy Young.

The following are *Update Newsletter* booklet publications. They are sold by fabric stores, machine dealers, and mail-order sewing supply companies. Or you can order individual titles for $3.95 each from *Update Newsletters*, 2269 Chestnut #269, San Francisco, CA 94123.

Advanced Serging Techniques, by Naomi Baker, 1988. Never-before-published serger techniques applicable to garment, craft, and decorating projects—serged-scalloped edging, serging padded paper, lace over fishing line and wire, three-dimensional flat and padded appliqué, plus double rolled-edge braid.

Beyond Finishing: Innovative Serging, by Naomi Baker, 1988. A concise, up-to-the-minute report on decorative serging—serged lace, fishline ruffles, tucked and rolled edges, and much more.

Serged Gifts, in Minutes! by Tammy Young, 1988. Nine charming projects that can be made in an hour or less—like a ruffled hanger, upholstered basket, or firewood carrier. No pattern purchases are required.

Serging Lingerie, by Naomi Baker, 1988. Learn to serge luxurious lingerie out of both knits and wovens. Edge-finishing and seaming are so easy that you can create beautiful basics or trousseau treasures quickly.

Serging Sweaters, by Naomi Baker, 1988. How to select the right fabrics, make your own pattern from a ready-made favorite, plus pro tips for cutting, seaming, and finishing.

Index

About the Authors

Naomi Baker is a nationally recognized serger authority who contributes monthly to *Update* newsletters, has authored several *Update* booklets, and has co-authored two previous Chilton books with Tammy Young. A home economics graduate of Iowa State University and former extension agent, she worked for Stretch & Sew for ten years. Naomi also has been an instructor for the Palmer/Pletsch Serger Workshops and provided extensive research for their early publications on serging. She specializes in technique research and development and is well known for her dressmaking skills.

Naomi has a sewing consulting and dressmaking business and appears across the country at special workshops and conventions. She lives and works in Springfield, Oregon, with her husband, three children, dog, huge fabric stash, and an enviable number of sergers and sewing machines.

Tammy Young has combined creativity and practicality in her writing and publishing career. Having worked for several years in the ready-to-wear fashion industry, she is known for her ability to translate retail trends into home-sewing techniques. Tammy is a home economics graduate of Oregon State University and a former extension agent and high school home economics teacher.

Tammy's office is located in San Francisco's Marina District, where she publishes *Update* newsletters and booklets, overseeing all facets of the business, including editing, illustration, layout, printing, and managing all other business details. She makes her home across the Golden Gate Bridge in Sausalito, and when her hectic schedule allows, travels stateside and abroad, frequently picking up trends and ideas for her publications.